MOBILITY MAT1

"*Mobility Matters* is a humorou ...ing
her vision little by little. Wheth ...with vision loss, knows someone who
does or who wants to understand more about those with vision impairment, this book
offers great insight."

-*Bettie Lou El Omari, certified life coach*

"The strength of *Mobility Matters* is the author's ability to be transparent with her readers
when facing her vision loss."

-*John Trotter, community researcher, South Asia*

"A clear testimony...*Mobility Matters* helped me to understand your journey in an
interesting, entertaining and sometimes humorous way. I couldn't put it down!"

-*Clyde Davis, senior pastor, Girard Alliance Church*

"I absolutely love your book!! I laughed, I cried, and so many times I said, 'Hey, I do
that, I did that, I felt that!' I can't wait to purchase a copy for my family to read."

-*Jennifer Sanderson, vision-impaired reader*

"*Mobility Matters* does a miraculous thing. It traces the heartbreaking progression of
vision and hearing loss in a way that ultimately feels hopeful. This book is a memoir
but reads like a novel. The reader wants to know what will happen next! All the elements
of a great story are here—drama, suspense, humor and memorable characters. It's one of
those books you are sorry to see come to an end."

-*Beckie Ann Horter, Christian blogger and editor for Proverbs 31 Ministries*

"You have the makings of a winner here...and a wonderful witness to God's love for us."

-*Janet Brantley, mystery and freelance writer*

"I couldn't wait to finish it! Incredibly moving and inspiring. Your characterization
of Bob and Julio made them jump off the page and I feel like I really know them."

-*Brittany Jo James, author of the thriller,* The Rebels

"A memoir that gives a great sense of the challenges the author faces...so honest,
sprinkled with cheeky humor throughout. Her story clearly shows that, for her, going
blind is a matter of retraining and she's determined to get it right."

-*Maribel Steel, writer and peer adviser at www.visionaware.org*

MOBILITY MATTERS: STEPPING OUT IN FAITH
Copyright © 2014 Amy L. Bovaird

ISBN-13: 978-1501036132
ISBN-10: 1501036130

Published by Amy L. Bovaird 634 Lake St. Girard, PA 16417 www.amybovaird.com

This book is nonfiction, based on events in my own life. The names of characters, except for family members, have been changed to protect the privacy of each individual. I've retained the names of places, for the most part, because they deserve high recognition for their excellence.

For more information on Amy Bovaird, please visit www.amybovaird.com.

Proofreader: RJ Thesman
Cover photos by Sarah Kay Gamble
Cover design and book layout by Heather Desuta

Printed in the United States of America.

MOBILITY MATTERS

Stepping Out in Faith

by

AMY L. BOVAIRD

To my sister, Carolyn.

*You have guided me through major life decisions
wherever I went and always reminded me to look UP,
and pray to see what God wants to do through me.
Thank you.*

INTRODUCTION

"No man is an island...entire of itself...."
John Donne

Mobility matters. Healthy people move a thousand times a day without giving it a second thought. They hop on busses, squeeze into their cars, or take walks when they feel like it. They dance, visit friends, go to parties, watch movies, or climb mountains. Nothing impedes them.

Not so for the vision-impaired. Restricted sight hinders movement. People with poor vision trip frequently, run into objects, or knock things over. When they're young, they get laughed at and made fun of. They're often called "clumsy" or "klutzy." As they get older, the jokes may become more intense. Fear of calling attention to themselves keeps them from doing the things they'd like to do, or from going places they'd like to go.

When that vision-impairment advances—as in my case with Retinitis Pigmentosa (RP)—a progressive hereditary retinal eye disease that begins with night blindness (usually discovered in early adolescence), narrows to tunnel vision, and ends in blindness or near-blindness—mobility becomes a serious issue.

In low light or darkness, the environment takes on a new, unpredictable, and often dangerous role. With Retinitis Pigmentosa, several things happen that "trick" my vision—an object, such as a tree, may suddenly pop up without warning, or another object, like a mud puddle, might exist outside of my field of vision. In the same way, it's easy to miss a step or fumble in a dark movie theater.

Over the years, I've heard a lot about what physically happens with this disease that one in 100,000 people live with. The rods and the cones break down and affect perception. Faulty nerve endings misconnect and over time, fall apart. My first retinal specialist explained my condition in these terms: living with RP is like a picture tube gradually wearing out on a television screen. Each eye has different "islands" of usable sight. Depending on the angle or lighting in which we see something, one island may compensate for a missing island in the other eye, and therefore, some days we can see better and thus move around more easily. Because this is a disease passed down through genes, there is no cure or operation to "fix" the faulty vision—although today retinal specialists are making great strides in genetic studies and a cure may come within our lifetime.

Early on, clumsiness affects general mobility. Later, it brings an RP sufferer to a crossroads. We must make more earth-shattering decisions, such as when is it no longer safe to drive? Should we use a cane or not? Some aren't frightened of these changes at all. They take on the responsibility of cane training matter-of-factly in order to stay independent. Others cannot bring themselves to pick up the phone to ask for help. Many don't even know where to seek information.

Obstacles abound: denial that they need a cane, fear of losing their independence and often, even their jobs. Other people's reactions enter into their decision. People fear being treated differently or looked down upon. They might feel more vulnerable or unsafe in public, as if, by using a cane, they broadcast their weakness and invite danger. Some might even begin to look at themselves in a different, less flattering or "less able" light. To many, taking up a red-and-white cane seems to point to a lifetime of limits and concessions. When someone with RP reaches this point, their world fills with the unfamiliar. One person told me it's like entering a foreign country where all the familiar cues are gone. For some, it's easier to stay at home in their own comfort zones, both mentally and physically, than to face and adapt to the challenges that cane training forces upon them.

Mobility matters because no one should be an island unto himself or herself. People fail to thrive when they're cut off from others or their interests. Life slows or may even come to a halt as discouragement sets in and individuals feel isolated. It's heartbreaking when someone gives up the quality of life to this disease out of fear—especially at a young age. Without interaction, there's no nourishment for our souls, and part of us dies, including the spirit. We become, to varying degrees, helpless.

Mobility matters because it gives independence back to that vision-impaired person. It lifts the wall of gloom that fragments a world into two factions: the sighted and the less-sighted or blind.

Mobility matters very much to me. I can't stop talking about the adventures in faith God set into motion in 2009. Starting with the right teacher, God transformed my mindset about using my cane. Almost from the start, I began to view my cane training as "faith training." Blindfolded, I envisioned myself "stepping out in faith" each time I left the house. My faith walk has lasted through two additional instructors and goes wherever I go every day. It all started out with that first hesitant step and sweep of my cane.

God purposely and perfectly paired me up with a no-nonsense mobility instructor whose personality complemented my learning style. Each session, as Bob challenged me to focus on my cane skill, I also gleaned an essential life lesson by watching him respond to others in our environment. He trained me to tune into my four senses to get information along with the cane. Bob knew when to skillfully intervene so that I wouldn't feel overwhelmed. At the same time he forced me to problem-solve unexpected challenges on my own. He relished the excursions he took me on. It showed in his speech and mannerisms, which, in turn, ignited my enthusiasm.

As a teacher, I knew what a fine line it took to balance expectation with performance. But he did it so well that I returned after every lesson bubbling over. "I crossed a busy city street alone!" or "Can you believe I ate at the bistro wearing sleep shades?" Like a magician, I held out my hand and demanded, "Ask me what denomination this bill is!" When I got it right, I crowed as if I had performed the best magic trick ever.

I can't wait to share the lessons I learned with you. Vision-impaired or sighted, take an arm for now, lean onto my optimism and faith. When you meet Bob, my instructor, you'll have to let go of me so I can pick up "my stick." Sorry, you might have to run alongside to keep up with the fast-paced nature of my training, but God will not leave your side. He's in the thick of it!

CONTENTS

"I, personally, prefer to use the word 'sight' rather than 'vision' because one can possess much vision with no sight; while the converse results in sighted people who are by no stretch of the imagination, visionaries. Blindness, to whatever degree, is simply the absence of sight; vision is quite another matter."

-Chet Smalley, Orientation & Mobility Specialist
Bureau of Blindness and Visual Services, Erie, PA

Chapter 1
STUMBLING IN THE DARK

I couldn't wait for my 30th high school class reunion.

Reconnecting with classmates excited me, not only because I hadn't seen them in so long but also because making that effort felt as if I were allowing certain pieces of a puzzle to slide into place. I needed to merge the person I used to be with the person I had become. My travels had changed me.

I had only one misgiving; how would I get around in the dark?

I'll just stay where it's well-lit, I told myself. *It'll be okay.*

Lorraine, one of the few friends I'd kept in contact with, picked me up in her van. When I got settled, I heard another voice coming from the dark form in the back seat.

Lorraine gestured. "You remember Carol, don't you?"

"Carol. Yes. I didn't see you there. How are you?"

I hadn't seen Carol since our tenth reunion.

"You both look so young and chic," I exclaimed, fiddling with my earrings and checking my lipstick.

"Yeah, real chic," Lorraine said with a smirk. "You notice we're all wearing Bermuda shorts, right?"

"Our clothes may look different but none of us has gained a pound since graduation. That's our story, and we're sticking to it," I said.

Carol reached over the seat to examine the jewelry on my arm. "I love that bracelet!"

"It's from Kenya." The tiny, luminescent pink shells coiled three times around my wrist. The bracelet felt light and summery on my arm, perfect for the occasion.

It was a treasured gift. After the village children sang to welcome me, a little girl had darted over to offer it. She hid behind a tree, peeking through her fingers to see my reaction. But I didn't tell Carol and Lorraine. Sometimes people don't know what to say when I talk about my life overseas. I've found it's best to keep my stories to myself.

The sweet perfume of honeysuckle and other mid-summer blooming flowers filled the air along with the laughter and stories my classmates told. I smelled the barbecued pig as I waited with the others, plate in hand.

Basking in the warmth of meeting up with so many classmates, I called out, "Hey, if you need someone to help at the next reunion, I'd be happy to join the committee."

"You're it!" Terry cried. "It's a done deal. No backing out."

Was I the only one? What did I get myself into?

We lingered over dinner, a casual affair, reminiscing over big football games, proms, wondering whatever happened to classmates who moved away, praising the best and bemoaning the worst teachers.

After dinner I stayed close to the picnic tables, which were lit up. Only when I needed to use the restroom did I venture away from them. I excused myself and made my way over to the port-a-johns at the far end of the property.

I fixed my eyes on the dim light, which kept wavering as it slipped in and out of my field of vision. It was like seeing a mirage.

You think it's real. You hope it's real. But you don't know until you get there if it's really what you think it is.

I prayed. What would I do? What would I say? Flickering lights often played tricks on my eyes. What if this light turned out to be the horseshoe pits?

My gaze shifted to the uneven ground. One leg caught on something. It buckled, and I stumbled and rolled.

It's a...bush. I jumped up and brushed off my clothing. I hoped no one saw that. Would I ever find this toilet?

An arm came out of nowhere to steady me. "It's me, Patty. Let me help you."

Thank you, Lord, I thought fervently, *You sent someone to guide me in the darkness.*

"Just a little further." My classmate linked arms with me, almost as if ... she knew. "I need to use it, anyway." She stopped and pointed. "That's the Women's. You can go first."

"Thanks."

I took a deep breath. *Nothing happened,* I told myself firmly. I hadn't embarrassed myself. I wasn't lost. I needed to take it easy.

Ten minutes later, we made our way back to the picnic tables, reminiscing about our school days. Too soon the long-awaited night was over, and we headed home.

I clasped my hands together. "Everything was perfect. I'm so glad I didn't miss this one."

That's when I learned my stumble in the dark had classmates buzzing, and not in a good way.

"I can't believe Tom really thought I was drunk." The heat rushed to my face as I sank back in my seat, covering my eyes with both hands. If only I could block out the words as easily as that. "He must have seen me stumble around in the dark and just assumed..."

"Appearances aren't everything," Carol consoled from the back seat.

But they are important when you're trying to impact people for Jesus.

"Besides, I told them you had an eye problem and couldn't see in the dark," Lorraine said, "so don't let them ruin your evening."

But for me, the evening *was* ruined. Even after thirty years, I still cared what my classmates thought about me. "I shouldn't have come—"

"Amy, you had a great time. I saw you chatting and laughing with everyone," Carol chided.

That was before I knew what they really thought.

I sighed. "Everything is distorted in the dark." As we rounded a curve, I reached for the dashboard.

"Your seatbelt," Lorraine reminded. "Amy, why don't you tell more people about your eyes?"

As I fastened my seatbelt, Carol leaned forward. She shook her head, "She shouldn't have to. It will be our secret, ladies. No one else needs to know."

Unsure how to respond, I kept silent, chafing at Carol's words. Why would I want to keep it a secret, as if I were hiding something bad about myself? I couldn't help what was happening to my eyes. It wasn't my fault both my parents carried faulty recessive genes and I inherited one from each.

Carol explained that she had suffered a serious, lengthy medical condition of her own. "It took time to recover, but that's no one's business but mine."

Was that why she was so sensitive to my situation?

It seemed Carol barricaded her private matters behind the high walls of the fortress where she lived. Funny I didn't see the irony in my own life when I bristled at her words that evening. I rarely confided in anyone about my vision problems. I, too, lived behind high walls.

CHAPTER 2
CONSIDERING NEW JOB CHALLENGES

A week later, I accepted a part-time teaching position at a Christian school not far from my house. Had I made the right decision?

Me, a Spanish teacher? But I hadn't spoken Spanish in years. Was it going to come back? I couldn't even roll my r's. No matter how many times I tried. I wasn't good at controlling kids either.

I had never been happier than when I left primary school and started teaching English to adults. All the control issues slipped into place. They wanted to learn. Moving ahead in their jobs depended on their success.

What would it be like to teach high school students? Demanding, certainly. In my new job, I'd be teaching Spanish II and III to them. The curriculum would be advanced. What if I forgot my grammar? Spanish III was a literature class. Teaching literature took language to a whole new level.

I started to doubt my abilities.

This was a mistake, I told myself over and over again. *I can't do it. I'll totally make a fool of myself.*

In the midst of my panic, a verse came to me. *I can do all things in Christ Jesus who strengthens me.*

I took a deep breath. *God, if this is Your way of providing for me, I'll do it. I'll trust You.*

A few nights later I dreamed that the elementary school kids ran wild in a small, open-air gymnasium in Colombia where I used to teach. One dark-haired six-year-old motioned them to follow her. They all ran behind the bleachers.

She peeked out and shouted, *"Su clase es muy fea."* She said my class was ugly, translation: boring.

I stood in the center of the room, pleading with them to come out and listen to the Spanish music. The tape recorder played and I started to clap. "Come on kids, *uno, dos, tres."*

The snippy little girl crossed her arms and refused to sing along.

"Niños!" I called to the children, "I know, lets—"

Suddenly I remembered I was supposed to teach the high school class. "Play with these balls for a little bit," I squeaked, throwing them some large plastic balls.

As happens in dreams, I magically arrived at the school in Pennsylvania. Disoriented, I ran down a long, dark hallway peeking into the classrooms—all in session. Where was my classroom? Where were my students?

Finally, at the end of the hallway, I saw them lounging by my closed door. "Sorry, I'm late!"

It was as if no one heard me. One of the high school boys pretended to be a car, rolling his r's flatly, like me.

"No, no, not that way," I said. *"Doble rr,* like this…*R con R cigarro—"*

A girl from my high school class peered at me, interrupting my tongue twister. "You're drunk. I'm going to tell the principal."

"No, wait, let me explain…."

Rrrrrinnng. It took me a minute to realize that I was sleeping and that sound was not the school bell but my alarm clock going off. My heart thumped in my chest. What a nightmare! *God, this isn't going to work.*

No way. Don't try to change my mind either!

That same afternoon the principal called me. She told me that the former Spanish teacher wanted to share her lesson plans with me and show me the book. "Let's schedule a time when you can meet. She's here now. Let me put her on the phone."

"Okay, hang on, let me get my calendar."

God, really? I guess You want me to take this job, huh?

The next afternoon, my friend, Mindy, and I met for lunch at Dairy Queen. She was the only one from our class besides Lorraine that I'd kept in contact with over the years.

In between bites of grilled chicken salad, I filled her in on the incident at the reunion and my newest job offer. I thought she'd make some joke about my stumbling to help me put it in perspective. But instead, she looked thoughtful. When she spoke, she focused on my new job.

"You'll do fine. You have excellent Spanish skills. Who cares if you can't roll your r's? Besides, Spanish is like anything else that's gotten rusty. It'll come back when you use it again. Meet with that teacher, get the book, and brush up on the grammar."

I nodded. If only it were that easy.

Mindy chased a stray piece of chicken into the honey mustard dressing and speared it with her fork. "Now what about that other job, the one you landed last May at the new college in town?"

I sighed. "Yeah, that's another problem. It's teaching Asian Studies. I'm not an expert. But the director thinks I have a good enough background to teach it since I lived in that part of the world for so many years."

"Good for you."

I took a sip of water. "She trusts that I'll do the class justice. It's a required course for freshmen. I'm still putting the syllabus together."

"You'll do a great job," she said, waving hello to someone she recognized at another table.

"I hope so."

Teaching at an American college intimidated me. Overseas, students respected their teachers. Here, college students seemed too informal.

I shared my fears with Mindy.

"You've got all that experience to fall back on. You lived there. You know about several cultures in Asia. It'll be a breeze for you."

"Yeah, you're right."

Mindy looked at her watch and snapped the plastic lid on her empty salad container. She looked over at me. "Just have fun with it. They're only freshmen."

"I know," I said, laughing. I stood up, smoothed my shorts and lifted my purse strap from the back of the chair.

As we walked into the bright sunlight, I shielded my eyes and stopped, waiting for them to adjust.

Mindy watched me. "Your classes are going to be a huge challenge. You'll be teaching little kids to high school to college-age, all at the same time." She whistled. "Wow!"

"I know." *They're all new situations, too.*

She backed out of the parking lot. "You know, Amy, if you're going to teach here, you're going to have to make some decisions. I'm going to tell you something that you probably don't want to hear. But you need to know."

I bit my lip. I hated it when she used that tone.

"You live in a small town now, whether you like it or not. If you want to keep a paying job here—you're not making much money off your writing— you're going to have to be careful of your reputation. You don't want to have your students thinking their teacher's the town drunk. You need to look into getting a cane or something."

"It's not *that* bad. No one knows."

"Amy, listen. It *is* that bad. People may not know *what* is wrong, but they definitely know something is. You're in denial."

I stiffly reached for the door handle and avoided her steady gaze. "What do you know about it?"

"I didn't want to tell you but at the reunion, some of our classmates asked me if you had Multiple Sclerosis because you were so unsteady on your feet. Another one thought you might have a neurological condition. And, of course, Tom asked me how long you'd had your 'drinking' problem."

I gasped. "Really? Tom didn't just think I was drunk that night. He thought I had a drinking problem? I can't stand it when people jump to conclusions."

"Did you hear what the others thought?" She tried to catch my eye. "When you don't tell people and they notice something out-of-sync, they're going to think: worst case scenario."

I flinched, one hand on the door handle, the other instinctively going to my forehead. Everything was so complicated!

"What happened at the reunion is going to happen again, but this time with more serious consequences. You can't afford to have anyone think the wrong thing. Call someone. Call that specialist who diagnosed you with your problem. Just. Get. Help."

Nice way to use my own words against me. Everything suddenly seemed overwhelmingly complicated. "Aaaaagggh, Min—"

She turned into my driveway and let the car idle. "Promise me you will."

"I don't know. It's...."

"Just do it."

Chapter 3
Leaving My Comfort Zone

"Mom, since I have these new teaching jobs, I probably need some kind of intervention," I said as casually as possible. "I need to know where I stand with my vision loss, don't you think?"

I half-hoped she didn't think so.

Mom looked up from the book she was reading. "That's a good idea. There's an eye doctor right on the corner of Main Street. You probably need to be referred to get help of any kind."

"Yeah."

I picked up the newspaper and sat down. Mom frowned. "Make an appointment. Do you need me to find the number in the phone book?"

I put down the paper and squared my shoulders. "No, I can do it."

A bell tinkled as I tripped over the threshold and into the office.

I liked Doc Pritchard on sight. He had big laugh lines around his eyes, and a shock of black unruly hair. The way he muttered to himself as he picked up

my file and hunted for a pen in his cluttered examining room reminded me of
an absent-minded professor. I finally realized which one—my high school biology
teacher. He continued gathering the few things he needed to examine me: a small
slender flashlight and eye drops, which he kept thumping against his hand.

"Darn lid is stuck."

I hid a smile as I watched him.

Picking up the flashlight, he faced me. "Okay, ready, let's take a look now."

After a speedy exam, Doc Pritchard said, "Your Retinitis Pigmentosa looks
pretty advanced. I don't even need to dilate your eyes. How 'bout that?"

"Yeah, how about that?" I tried to smile. But inwardly I tensed, wondering
what was so obvious that he didn't need drops to see.

He set the small flashlight aside, rolled his chair back and studied me.
"I have no problem recommending you to Rita at the BBVS. She'll fix you right up."

He gave me a lopsided grin, and I almost expected him to hand me a sucker.
Instead he handed me a phone number and curled my fingers around it.

"The BBVS?"

"Rita is a caseworker at the Bureau of Blindness and Visual Services."

I grimaced. "Right."

"You'll like her. She's great."

I figured I'd like her. I just didn't want to *need* her.

"Officially, we'll have to sort out your field of vision." He made a face and
mumbled, "More fun paperwork." I chuckled. Apparently, Doc Pritchard was
not a fan of paperwork. "But for now, since you say you can't hear worth a
darn," he said, smiling to lighten the complaint, "you need a hearing test. It's
possible you have Usher's Syndrome, which goes along with RP."

"Usher's?"

"There are a couple of types of Usher's." He rubbed his chin. "The first is
predominately found in babies. There's another kind that appears around
adolescence. What I'm guessing you may have is a third, less common type

they're discovering which comes later in life." He tapped the file folder with his pencil. "Like your vision loss, it's progressive," he added gently.

"So…I could become deaf, too?"

"Well…" Doc Pritchard bobbed his head back and forth, noncommittally. "First we need to get you to an Ear Nose and Throat specialist and test for it. No need to panic."

"Of course," I said quickly. "I've actually heard of Usher's. I read about it when I was diagnosed."

"Call Rita and we'll get the exams set up, so you'll have some answers, and maybe new hearing aids, by the time your classes come around."

Hearing aids? I was only forty-eight years old.

Rita got me on the caseload in record time. I had a field of vision exam, met with an audiologist, and then the ENT specialist. With the audiologist's report of forty-five percent hearing loss in one ear and forty in the other, the specialist confirmed Doc Pritchard's suspicions.

"It's likely to be Usher's Syndrome, Type III." As with my initial diagnosis of RP, he couldn't say how fast I would lose my hearing. "It's different with everyone."

My audiologist, Holly, couldn't be any nicer. She made the wax imprints to prepare me for hearing aids. "You have such tiny ear holes."

"Really?" I was thrilled at the big compliment. I might not be able to see well, but I certainly had *dainty* ear holes. Hearing aids might not be that bad. "When will they be ready?"

"I'd say the whole process will take a month or so."

A month? I gulped. My new classes started in two weeks.

Chapter 4
Braving Dark Fears

"There." The hum of the copy machine went silent after the last staple was punched into place. I gathered the papers together, packed them into my briefcase, and zipped it shut. I left the small campus, my mind on the lecture I was preparing about the first chapter of the book. I'd be ready for next week.

While I prepared for the Asian Studies course independently, I attended face-to-face meetings to organize myself for the academic year at the Christian Academy. In mid-August, the faculty members en masse attended a one-day workshop in Pittsburgh, and I made friends with a few teachers. At the end of an exhausting day, Mrs. Johns, who taught English and History to the high school students, and I talked non-stop in the back of the bus. I felt confident God had hand-placed me in this job and equally confident of my Spanish again.

At the Teacher Breakfast, the first staff get-together, the principal introduced me to the all-women faculty. For me, it passed in muffled disorientation. My hearing difficulties set me at the fringe of the discussion. While I caught various bursts of talk and laughter, the details blurred. I smiled throughout and prayed no one would ask me any questions. Had my hearing diminished that much in the three years since I last taught? Would this happen in my classroom?

All of our teacher meetings passed in the same muffled blur. I tried not to panic.

As the time to teach drew closer, I reminded myself how the principal and I had prayed for God's will during the initial job interview. I had confided in Mrs. Curtis from the onset about my vision and hearing difficulties, and she took them in stride.

God was providing for me. Silently, I ticked off the reasons why I knew this job was from God: the school was close enough for me to walk to work. Spanish was my favorite language and my proficiency had returned. Language teaching was my specialty. The textbook, while dated, was well-organized and easy to understand. Mrs. G, the former Spanish teacher, had a bank of quizzes and tests already made up. She now took on Computer and High School Bible class but would also teach Spanish to the elementary school students. I think she took these classes as a special favor to me.

God never leads you to a challenge without providing you a way to accomplish it, right? I highlighted a scripture in my Bible in Psalms: *I will guide you along the best pathway for your life.*

Clasping that promise, I tried to push away my newfound fears of teaching a foreign language when I couldn't hear…any language. That fright had suddenly overshadowed my initial concern about coping with vision problems.

One day shortly before I started teaching, Mom and I shared tea and biscuits. As I sipped the hot tea, I said, "Mom, I might not see straight down the path God put me on right now, but I can definitely see how He cleared the way for me to move."

"You're a good teacher. You've won a lot of awards over the years," she remarked.

I wasn't referring to awards so much as the people God had placed in my life to help me succeed, one of whom was Julio—my confidant, my sparring partner, and a mentor in many areas of my life. He lived on the West Coast, but that didn't stop him from calling me several times a day to make sure I'd be ready for my classes.

Mom stood up and held out her hand for my cup. "Are you and Julio still working on your lectures on that computer program every night?"

"Skype? Yes. He spends hours online with me making sure I understand what I'll be teaching. That's a God thing. Plus, he knows Spanish and can help me with the high school students."

Julio and I shared a history that went all the way back to 1988 in Indonesia where we both taught English to a select group of Indonesia's best students and prepared them to study abroad. Though our lives intersected a mere year, we remained lifelong friends. I moved back to the States while Julio went on to earn his Master's degree in International Affairs with a concentration in Southeast Asia, and a PhD in Anthropology. He finished his dissertation on a mining camp in remote Indonesia. Over time, Julio developed cultural insights and a deep understanding of that part of the world.

My opposite in personality, the Indonesians dubbed him my "nice enemy." His sarcasm and quick-witted responses sometimes deflated me. But he also had a knack for talking sense into me and keeping my problems in perspective. Even when I wanted to cry, he made me laugh instead.

It was no coincidence he had expertise in both subjects I was teaching.

"I'm so grateful I'm home again and that we can share what God is doing in our lives. He's brought me here so we can be together. Now that my money has run out, God is providing."

A slow contented smile formed on Mom's face as she rinsed the dishes. "I waited for many years for you to come home from overseas."

"I know, Mom. Thanks."

❖ ❖ ❖

A student raised his hand. "Umm, Mrs...Oh, yeah, *Profesora* ... uh ... Bufaird, are we supposed to get Spanish names, too?" Bov-aird, like air. Should I draw his attention to the fact he mispronounced my name? Just let it go today.

"Si. Tengo una lista aquí."

"Huh?"

I switched to English at their blank stares. "I have a list here. I'm sure you can distinguish between the girls and boys names." I kept it light and fun.

After each one chose a name, I took out a red sponge apple. "Now we'll practice your Spanish names. *Tiro el peloto así,* " I said tossing the ball gently to the newly-named Pedro. He looked surprised but caught it. "Now you throw it to a classmate and say their new name."

"María."

She caught it, and I nodded for her to choose the next one.

The activity went as planned until a few students started whipping the ball to classmates.

"*Suavamente.* Easy," I admonished.

When I saw one shy female student cover her face to protect herself, I realized she wasn't enjoying our activity anymore. "Okay, stop." I reached for the ball. "Enough name practice for today. Now everyone choose a partner. Got one?" I indicated the remaining students. "You three can work together."

I passed out a two-page biographical handout of me written in simple past tense Spanish. The students were to read and discuss the content.

Their jaws dropped, and they looked at each other in confusion as they flipped the paper over several times. Finally one girl raised her hand. "*Profesora* Bervard, what if my partner can't understand? It will take *all day* for me to explain it." She looked falsely apologetic. "We only have half an hour."

There is only one r in my name. She really massacred it. I'd have to draw the students' attention to the proper pronunciation of my name if this continued. "That's okay, let's see what you can get done if you start now."

She gave me a bright smile. "We'll need dictionaries then." To my dismay, she walked over to the shelf and started passing out large hardcover dictionaries.

Not quite what I expected for the first day.

My Spanish III class went a little better. With only one student, a clever one at that, we moved smoothly from one activity to another. On a hunch, I passed out the same background of me in Spanish. Piedad also struggled with it though she worked hard to translate it until the bell rang.

They're still translating. Did I do that in high school? The students obviously spoke a lot more English than Spanish in the classroom. I glanced at my watch. *I need to get to the college.* I gathered my books, shut off the light, and headed for the parking lot where my brother waited.

My schedule at the college fell on Tuesdays and Thursdays. We started classes on Thursday. That day, I set everything up and fiddled with the sophisticated computer equipment, sliding in the CD with my infographics and lecture notes. Soon, the students arrived.

When I explained the breakdown of grades, it didn't seem to go over well. "You mean if we're late, you'll deduct points?"

"Yes, that's correct."

One disgruntled female said, "Well, You know, there are extenuating circumstances."

I have to be strong and confident. I smiled. "Not in this course." I continued. "This is an Asian Appreciation class. That means that we're going to look at the wonderful cultural elements various societies have and learn about their belief systems."

Agnes, the outspoken student who challenged me earlier, said, "Yeah, in China they kill their daughters. I saw a program about that."

"In China, they also have a long history of ingenuity."

"Yeah, if you're a man. 'Cuz if you're a woman, they're going bind your feet and cripple you."

The class tittered.

"That is part of their history. We'll discuss that. But we're going to look beyond the stereotypes to better understand what shaped their societies and how the geographical elements contributed." I warmed to my topic.

Someone groaned.

Then it happened. I bent over to pick up my textbook, hit my head on the table, which sent both my glasses and the book sailing. As I bent over to feel for my glasses on the carpeted floor, someone handed me the book. "Thank you," I said amid the laughter. I couldn't tell if they were laughing at me or with me.

I felt my forehead. I knew at the touch, I had a swollen goose egg in the middle of my forehead. I was used to it, but not in front of a new class of seemingly hostile students.

"Funny way to start out, huh?" I wet my lips. "Why don't you introduce yourselves and share one unique aspect so that we can remember you." I sat down to take notes. When we finished, I wanted to show a PowerPoint presentation on the computer. But nothing came on the screen.

One of the quieter students spoke. I couldn't even tell where the voice came from.

I looked around the room and said, "Could whoever just spoke repeat himself?"

A male student in the back of the room called out, "Did you log in?"

Some of the students laughed. Was he making fun of me? Of course I knew to log in.

"Yes. At the start of class. I did." I hoped I didn't sound as flustered as I felt.

"At the start of class? That's the problem. It logs you out after ten minutes. You have to sign in again."

"Oh, oh. Okay."

It took ten minutes to get the information on the screen. Dead time. Never good in a classroom situation, especially at the college level.

"Make sure to take notes," I instructed. "This information won't be available later."

"Oh, man. Do we have to write all that?"

In my Spanish II class, we followed the vocabulary and exercises in the book. My biggest problem was hearing some of the more reticent students. Though I monitored the classroom by walking around, I still couldn't hear if some of the girls gave me the correct answer or how they pronounced the words.

I have to admit sometimes I fudged and pretended I'd heard.

Each student sat at an old-fashioned single desk-chair combination with a black rack underneath to hold books. These desks were situated in neat rows. The center of the room held a cement column. When I monitored my students, it seemed I played peek-a-boo around the column to see everyone. The room—better suited to a smaller Sunday school class—cramped my usual style.

Monitoring and my impaired vision didn't match up well in this classroom situation.

When I tried to quietly move between the rows to monitor written work, I tripped over some of the students' books that spilled out into the aisle from the bottom racks.

"Ooof!" I grunted after one such incident.

"Ow!"

"Ay, Lo siento, Raquelita," I apologized, adding the 'ita,' an endearing term, while I patted the student's long hair which I'd yanked when I collided with her.

"Did I break your *cabeza*?"

"My *what*?"

"Your head." I knocked on my own in a comical way to show how hard it was.

Her face turned red, and she slid down in her chair at the unwanted attention.

"Students, that's what happens when your books are in the aisle. Please ensure you store them properly in the rack under your desk."

I inspected the rest of the rows, tapping books with the tip of my shoe and making the students laugh.

At times, I felt like a vulture circling through the room seeking out targets to attack. Although I didn't pull someone's hair every day, I stumbled frequently. One day I even ran into the cement column. I thought for sure I'd see blood and have to get stitches. But I didn't. God protected me and we got through such moments.

While I struggled to monitor my foreign language classroom at its basic level, I also struggled with some of the content. I had one student who challenged me when I attempted to teach direct and indirect objects.

Suddenly, I doubted myself. Was I teaching it correctly or incorrectly?

I had no idea what the students thought of my knowledge of the target language, my tripping around the room or why I constantly asked them to repeat themselves. When I asked them to repeat themselves, they probably thought they made a mistake. I couldn't talk about my vision or hearing issues. I believed that I would lose my authority. So I kept my lips sealed and prayed harder.

God, I need my hearing aids, I prayed. *I can't stand it! I do trust I'm in the right job but it's really hard.*

Each night Julio grilled me on my classes. While I voiced my newfound insecurities, he poked fun at my classroom catastrophes and I laughed, imagining myself through the eyes of my students. On bad days, I made a note to find my framed Outstanding Teacher Performance awards from a former teaching job. I sometimes wondered if I were the same teacher.

❖ ❖ ❖

Tuesdays rolled around quickly. Before long, we had reached the start of our third week at the college. Since students earned points for attendance, I wanted to make sure I marked them "present" on my roster. Quickly scanning the room, I accounted for all but one of them. "Tanya?"

I waited for a few seconds and called louder. "Tanya?" If she would only raise her hand as requested so even when I couldn't hear her, I might see her. *Ideally.*

No answer.

I tapped the desk with my pencil. "Is Tanya here? Can everyone be quiet now? It's time to start class."

The noise didn't stop completely. I didn't know whether my students were disregarding my authority more as the weeks wore on, or if they were just being typical American college students. Could it be they picked up on my hearing problems and were taking advantage of me?

"If Tanya doesn't answer, she'll be marked absent for today and lose those points. What a shame."

"I'm here!" She practically yelled it.

"Okay, that's all I wanted to know."

A headache started rolling in.

Toward the end of the hour, I reminded the students their outside assignments were due. "Leave them on my desk." I pointed to an empty space on the table in front of me. "Once you do that, you're free to take a break. When we get back, we'll have our lecture." I yawned as I gathered up some photographs and bound them with a rubber band.

As the students dispersed, from the corner of my eye I saw one of my more unpleasant students heading in my direction. She marched over to me as if to war. "Ms. Bovard, we need to talk. I *have* to have an extension."

"I'm sorry, Agnes. I heard you say your husband was ill. But you have had five days to do this assignment. It's due today."

Her eyes bulged, and her top and bottom teeth slowly separated as she let out a loud, "HUH?

I picked up the photographs and straightened the corners, my stomach suddenly clenching.

She folded her arms over her chest, looking determined. "I was so busy taking care of him that I couldn't even do my in-class assignment, let alone anything else."

I bit my lip, wishing I were anywhere but at my desk facing her. "We talked about deadlines on our first day of class. Sorry about your husband. But that doesn't change my policy."

"You crummy...." I flinched as the pitch of her voice rose and she cursed between cutting accusations. The remaining students froze in mid-action, all eyes on the two of us.

My head pounded. I'd had bad teaching days but nothing like this. "That's not appropriate language."

"I don't think you understand my situation," she shouted, emphasizing each word. Her face contorted as she leaned toward me, so close that drops of spittle hit me.

She became a drill sergeant and me, the lowly recruit.

"Agnes, I'm so sorry." How could I not be when she was in such a dither... all for five measly points. "This policy is...."

She jabbed a finger inches away from my face and screeched, "Don't you patronize me!"

A student from another class peeked in the half-open door, stared and waited for my response.

It took me so long to clear my throat I wondered if I could even speak. I coughed. "Agnes, this assignment isn't worth that many points."

She slammed her fist on my table. "You know nothing. Your stupid policies. I haven't left my house in four days!" She clenched a fist and shook it violently.

I quickly backed up against the whiteboard.

My knees shook. Agnes let out a long hissing breath, much like an old-fashioned steam heater. *Sssssss*. She let her fist drop and seemed to be looking for something—I suspected my grade book—whatever it was, she didn't find it. In a fit of rage, she grabbed my textbook and whipped it at the wall. It landed with a thud and slid to the floor. "My husband's been deathly ill, and you want me to fail this course. You want to give me a big fat zero."

My stomach was in knots. I tried to get her to keep things in perspective. "Agnes, listen. It's just one assignment."

My students, along with students in the business course from the next room over, sat on the floor near the door whispering to each other. Whose side were they on? Would anyone defend me? They looked curious—none seemed to want to stop the drama. Of course, that was *my* job.

I let out a shaky breath, wringing my hands together as I tried to think.

Agnes's nostrils flared, and she narrowed her eyes. "You don't know how to teach." She continued with deliberate cruelty. "No one here even likes this class!"

I blinked back tears. Do not cry. Do *not* cry. I am the instructor here. She's bullying me. I have to get the control back. This isn't my first year of teaching. It's my twenty-second. God did not give me a spirit of timidity. He gave me *strength*. I pushed back my nerves and stared her down. "Are you speaking for everyone?"

Without responding, she stomped out of the classroom and slammed the door. It shook from the impact, and I wondered if it would fall off the hinges.

What a crisis!

I walked away from the whiteboard. This definitely called for a time-out to pull myself together.

"Everyone, take five." I pulled the door open to let them know they should leave. I didn't know if they'd take five or ten or the whole class session nor did it matter at that moment. After the last student exited, I deliberately left the door open to show that I retained control. No secrets. No tears.

God, is it ever going to get any better? I can't believe I'm doing such awful teaching. I hate this job! I can't see. I can't hear. Look what kind of problems my hearing loss causes. I can't imagine what the students think of me now. How can I teach them today?

A few minutes later, a first-year student entered. She walked over to my desk and addressed me politely, "Miss Bovaird, are you okay?"

Finally a student who pronounced my name properly. "Yes, I'm fine." It wasn't true, but what else could I say?

"Agnes should be kicked out. It's not your fault." She smiled at me. "You have funny stories. I love your class," she said, taking her seat.

I think God sent that girl to me. Her words spurred me on to set up the lecture. With the exception of Agnes, everyone returned. For the first time, they quietly took notes.

That night I went home and dug through my Bible, looking for some encouragement. Millions of pins seemed to prick the back of my eye. Of course, stress. Through the pain, I pressed on until I had a verse to fall back on. *The LORD will guide you always; he will satisfy your needs...and will strengthen your frame.*

I printed it out, the tears falling onto my computer keys. Taped on my computer screen, this scripture would help me through the next seven weeks.

A couple of days later the phone rang. It brought good news. "My hearing aids are ready? Great!"

I immediately felt my spirits lift after the stress-filled three weeks of work. Things were sure to improve now. I could hardly sleep in anticipation. Would it make a difference?

In a matter of minutes after I arrived at the office, the gentle technician slipped in the second hearing aid. She did a few evaluations to test my hearing with them and said, "That's you, now."

Although the hearing aids didn't come from the technician personally, a lump filled my throat, and I could hardly get the words out at the gift of hearing she gave me. "Holly, thank you so much."

She looked over at me, surprised. "Just doing my job."

I took the black velvet hearing aid case from her outstretched hand and whispered, "Thank you," again. "This is life-changing."

By the time evening came around, I wanted to rip them out of my ears. When I climbed the steps to my apartment, the jarring footstep on each stair sounded like it came from a giant instead of a ninety-eight pound girl. The voice on the radio hit me as if someone shouted through a loudspeaker right next to me. The ticking of the clock sounded like someone slamming down a hammer at precise and even intervals. At 10:00, I took them out and finally got a break. I rubbed my ears and lay down wondering how I'd stand it for the rest of my life.

The next day at the academy—a Friday, I remember it well—My Spanish II students took their first exam. The amplification in these tiny, sophisticated mechanisms so sensitized my hearing that when the students turned their papers over, it even magnified the rustling of papers.

It blew me away.

Thank you, Jesus. I closed my eyes. *I have my life back.*

Chapter 5
Don't Say "Blind"

Standing back, I gave my apartment a final walk-through. With my toe, I straightened a small throw carpet between the living room and kitchen. A stray dish towel cluttered the counter. That needed to go in the wash. The cupboard door under my sink hung askew. I scrounged in a drawer for a screwdriver to tighten it.

In the living room, I smoothed the bare cushion of my loveseat. The throw covering never came off unless it was washday or company visited because it served as Buddy's bed. At least the cushions didn't appear to have any dog hair.

"Stay down," I ordered when Buddy looked longingly at his bed.

He knew that tone. But ever hopeful for a change of heart, his tail thumped against the floor. Seeing me leave, his tail slowed down and stopped all together. He looked pitiful stretched out on the hard floor.

"Okay, this is as good as it's going to look. I'm ready for Bob."

If only I had something other than water to offer. "I should've made some cake or cookies," I muttered.

But this was not a social call. It was my first meeting with Bob, my mobility specialist. Rita, my caseworker, kept telling me how "helpful" it would be for me to talk with him. She pushed me into agreeing to meet Bob.

Nearly 7:00. He'll be here any minute. I listened for my doorbell, but heard a shout from the stairs instead. "You have someone here to see you," Mom called. Her voice sounded funny.

Drat! I forgot to tell Bob to come around back to my place. He must have come to the front of the house.

"On my way, Mom."

There, just inside our front door, stood Bob.

As I came toward him, I noticed two things in quick succession. In his right hand he held a long red and white cane. Then, when he looked toward me, I saw his eyes focused somewhere over my shoulder.

Bob was blind.

My mobility specialist was *blind?*

Oh no. Mom had said, 'You have someone here to *see* you.' I hope that didn't offend him.

I observed him more closely. He was a giant of a man. He wore a Captain's cap just like Dad always did. Graying, slightly unruly hair peeked out from underneath.

"Bob Braniff," he said, extending his hand in my general direction. He had a firm handshake.

"Hi, I'm Amy," I said automatically.

I didn't know what to say next. What do you do when a blind person comes into your house? How would we get up to my place? I eyed his cane. Could he tap his way through our house? What would I have to do? Would I just give him instructions? I couldn't just sit him down in my mother's living room with the television blaring. My mother's hearing was worse than mine. My mind raced, trying to think of what to do next. He continued to wait patiently at the front door.

In a panic to fill the silence, I said the first question that popped into my head. "Bob, how did you get here?"

"My driver. He's in the car."

"Oh. Should I invite him in?"

"Not necessary. He's perfectly fine where he is."

Why didn't Bob tell me he was blind?

"Sorry, I have my own place. Right now, we're in my mother's living room. Um, if you go straight ahead…." Can I say straight ahead to a blind person? How will he know where that is? Bob extended his cane. "You'll find some stairs we need to climb." Should I tell him how many? Would that insult him? I didn't want him to fall. That would be terrible if he broke a leg in our house.

I needn't have worried. Bob had no difficulty following me.

He banged the cane against each step as he climbed. Oh dear. Mom was particular about her house. My dad built those steps.

"Then, uh, there will be a small hallway. After a few steps, we'll turn… left…that's my bedroom. From there, we'll go straight through to my kitchen."

I seemed to be guiding him okay. I didn't want him to trip on anything. Thank God, I'd cleaned my place up.

"Okay, we're in my kitchen. Make sure you turn…ah, right, because if you turn left, you'll fall down some stairs. We don't want that." I hope he didn't think I was making a bad joke at his expense.

"We certainly don't." His voice boomed in my small apartment.

I spied the throw rug between the kitchen and living room and had visions of Bob's cane getting tangled in the cloth, which would trip him. "'Scuse me, Bob," I said, scooting around him to snatch it up. Whew! Just in time.

"Now, you'll find a large tan love-seat." Why on earth did I mention the color? He can't see the color. Rub it in, Amy. This guiding stuff sure wasn't easy. "You can have a seat there."

Just as he lowered himself onto the cushion, I caught a glimpse of Buddy's tail. "Oh, uh, that's uh, my, my…."

Oh my gosh, he just sat on my dog.

Bob jumped up. "Seems to be something…."

"Yeah, that's my dog. Sorry. He usually sleeps there." Bad boy! I'm sure as soon as I left, he jumped onto the sofa. I reached for his collar to lead him down. "Buddy, c'mon." The dog made himself heavy and stayed put. He wouldn't budge unless I gave him a treat. He'd trained me well.

I dashed into the kitchen to get one and tossed it on the floor.

Buddy eyed the treat and decided on the trade-off. He jumped off the loveseat to retrieve it. I brushed any stray hairs off the cushion. "Okay, Buddy's off the sofa. Now you can sit down."

Bob took his seat and reached out a friendly hand in front of him. The dog leaned forward for a head rub. How did Bob know where Buddy was?

"What did you call this fella'?"

"Buddy." I clapped my hands to get the dog's attention. "C'mon. Sorry, you'll have to go behind the line." That was my term for the dog gate at the far side of the kitchen.

My intention was to get him anywhere out of the way so Bob wouldn't trip over him. With that task done, I called in to Bob. "Would you like a glass of ice water?" I tried to make it sound inviting instead of the only drink I had to offer.

"Water, now that would be perfectly splendid. However, I really must use your bathroom first."

I have to direct him again? Come on, it's no big deal. "Yeah, sure."

I walked ahead of Bob, turning back to give instructions as I guided him to the bathroom across the hall.

Maybe I'd better wait to show him the way back.

But Bob never looked for me, not even once. Why would he? He couldn't see me. Dumb!

He looked as if he knew exactly where he needed to go.

It seemed rather underhanded of me to follow him since I didn't make myself known. I wondered if Bob knew I trailed behind. I hoped not. Maybe he'd think I didn't trust him in my house.

"I see you made it back all right," I said when he sat down."Ready for your water?"

"I am, indeed."

I carefully placed the glass in his hand. "A tall glass for a taller gent," I said, trying to put us both at ease.

He took a sip of water. "So Amy, can you tell me a little about yourself?"

It wouldn't do at all to sit beside him on a *loveseat* so I pulled over a chair and sat directly across from him. We talked about my job and prior travels. He was so attentive that when he eased into the topic of vision, I explained what I knew about Retinitis Pigmentosa. I almost forgot it wasn't a social visit until he said, "Perhaps the best solution is to simply tell people that you are blind."

"I'm not *blind*. I have a vision problem." I glared at him—not that he would notice.

"Okay." He nodded, not at all put out by my response. "Let me explain what I mean by 'blind.' Blindness is a continuum. Not every blind person has lost all his vision. Some people still retain some residual vision, but not enough to drive or do what many others take for granted. These people are legally blind."

He stopped, perhaps to let his words sink in.

I didn't know what to say. I couldn't get past his earlier advice of what I should tell others.

"Okay, let me give you an example. For someone who is legally blind, an object at twenty feet away appears to be much farther away. It's the equivalent to what others would see at two hundred feet. If you want to talk in degrees, a legally blind person has less than ten percent of vision remaining. Sometimes blind people can only see light but not shapes. What can you see?"

"A lot." Arms tightly crossed, I pressed my lips together.

Neither of us immediately spoke. I finally gave in because I don't like long silences.

"I don't know, Bob. My problem is more what I don't see. Objects in clear sight vanish—my keys, change, or my cell phone. I guess that happens to everyone. But lately, something weird is going on. If I'm reading, printed words will break up and disappear, and then fall into place a minute later. It's maddening. I don't even see my dog half the time." I stopped. Didn't he just sit on my dog? He couldn't see my dog at all. Why did I give that example?

"Go on," he encouraged, not seeming to notice my blunder.

Once I started, the floodgate opened.

"It's like my eyes constantly play tricks on me. Objects suddenly pop into my path."

Bob sat forward, really listening. "What kind of objects?"

"I don't know, like trash cans, poles in the supermarket, cupboard doors, small boxes. Anything higher than my elbow and lower than my thigh causes danger. I get bumps, scrapes, bruises, and sometimes even stitches."

He nodded. "Not very pleasant scenarios. Not at all."

"Bob, I run into tables and open cupboard doors and miss steps. I walk into walls and bump my head on my breakfast bar."

"Are you legally blind?"

"I'm not sure." Twenty years earlier, when I was diagnosed, the doctor said as much. But people who lose their vision gradually can get by for a long time. We keep adapting. Suddenly a big chunk of vision disappears. After everything I'd said to Bob, I still couldn't admit it.

"From what you tell me, I'd say you could benefit from using a cane. Have you ever thought of that?"

"You mean a *blind* man's cane?"

Did I just say that out loud? I can't believe I blurted that out! "Bob, I didn't mean…um, I meant like blind in a good way, well, it probably didn't come out that way..." I was just making it worse. "Sorry, I don't need a cane. I'm just clumsy. I never look where I'm going."

If only we could start this conversation over again. Better yet, maybe he'd drop this terrible subject all together.

He didn't sound upset. "It's called a 'mobility cane.' Others may call it 'a red and white cane.' But you'll learn all that. Would you be willing to try it out for a session, perhaps around your neighborhood just to get a feel for what it's like?"

Bob's correction and pleasant voice grated on my nerves. But at least he wasn't angry even though I had been so rude. Maybe I owed him something. "How long is a session?"

"Oh-h-h, an hour or so would be enough, I believe."

Where other people could see me? No way.

"You wouldn't even need to wear sleep shades—unless you wanted to," he cleverly added.

"Sleep shades?"

"Yes, indeed. These are black shades like you wear on an airplane to get some shut-eye. Although I've never had a need for them myself," he added, chuckling. It was the first casual remark he'd made in reference to his vision.

His humor caught me off guard, and I snickered.

"The sleep shades are great for blocking out the light. The real *benefit*," he enthused "is that you get simulated practice under the same environmental conditions as when you absolutely need your cane. Like at night."

But I would look weird.

"How about it?" His voice took on a stronger, eager edge, like he wanted to seal the deal.

"All right." I let out a long sigh. "I can at least try it."

Bob winked as if he were certain all along that he'd win me over. He bent down and felt around his feet, lifting a large black nylon bag I hadn't even noticed him carry in. How could I not have noticed that big bag? "Superb." He smiled confidently. "Now what size do you think you'll need?"

"Size? What do you mean?" Would I need other equipment, like special shoes?

"I'm referring to the length of the cane you'll need," he explained. "How tall are you?"

"Five foot one."

"Fifty-two inches would be about right then." He rummaged through his bag and extracted a folded cane, then slid his hand down the length of that section. "Yes, this is the one." He seemed to be feeling for something else. "This cane has a marshmallow tip. That's because it's small and shaped like a marshmallow. Here, feel it."

I tentatively reached out and slid my fingers over the smooth white tip.

He poked around again, his fingers feeling for a specific texture. In spite of myself, I was intrigued. He withdrew another cane. "Now this one has a more rounded tip. It's called a gliding hook tip." He held out the bottom to me. "Feel the difference?"

"Hmm."

He took out another. "This one has a pencil tip. Feel how long and narrow it is." He surfaced again with yet another cane and tip. "This particular one comes with a roller ball tip. It's perfectly round. See how smooth that is. It just rolls down the sidewalk."

I noticed his voice took on that admiring tone sports car aficionados use as they describe the attributes of a 1965 Corvette. They rattle off any number of details about it. I almost asked how much mileage he thought this particular cane would get.

He explained how each cane was divided into four sections. "See this?" He stretched an elastic cord outside the red casing. "This enables the user to fold the cane up into neat sections. Isn't that nifty?" Bob's eyes sparkled.

For a moment, I softened toward him.

Bob, the Cane Man.

"...So don't worry so much about blindness. Don't let your sight or lack thereof define you. It's only one of many characteristics that make you who you are."

The good feelings I had toward Bob vanished when I heard that one word—blindness.

His voice took on a persuasive tone. "Want to try a few canes?"

And go for a spin? "Ah, well, hmm...." I couldn't get out of the situation without being downright rude.

"Try the fifty-two inch," Bob said, deftly unfolding it. "Are you right-handed or left?"

"Right."

He placed it in my hand, straightening my thumb and index finger while curling my others around the top. "Don't worry about this elastic strap. It's necessary to store the cane compactly when you aren't using it. For now, let it hang. Just walk around the room," he encouraged. "Back straight, head up."

Was I a model now?

"Is that the right length? Would you like to try a shorter one? I have an excellent forty-nine inch. Lighter weight, too."

"All right."

He set me up with it. "Go," he said, giving me a little push. "Wait. Sweep it back and forth."

I inched into the kitchen. My fingers already felt numb from the strain. Buddy looked on curiously from behind his boundary line.

Bob continued his push for practice. "Shall we venture out to the rest of your house?"

I groaned, inwardly. In our test drive—I mean, walk—we explored the house and even made it into the basement where Mom washed clothes.

"Mrs. Bovaird, Amy's doing a great job!" Now how did he know anyone was there? And how did he know that it was my mom?

She looked startled. Whether that was due to the unfamiliar canes or something else, I wasn't sure. Mom sometimes seemed uncomfortable with unfamiliar faces in the house. Since my father had passed away three years earlier, not many new people came around.

When we got back to my place, I checked the time. "Bob, it's been way over an hour. Your poor driver." What would he do in the car for all that time? How could we be so thoughtless?

"Yes, I believe it's time for me to take my leave," Bob said in the particularly formal way he had of speaking. "Now, let's schedule your neighborhood session."

My stomach tensed. I could do without that session. "I'm kind of busy at work now. How about if I give you a call and we can schedule it?"

Bob looked disappointed. He shook his finger at me, "Now see to it that you don't forget."

"I won't."

As soon as Bob left, I picked up my cell phone and punched in some numbers. Looking back on that moment, I find it odd that I didn't call any of the friends I grew up with. Instead, I waited for someone to answer clear across the United States in California.

Like me, Julio had moved back home to be near family.

"Hurry up, answer." I drummed my fingers on the computer desk as I waited.

When he picked up, he didn't mince words. "So how did 'the meeting' go?"

"He didn't even *tell* me that he was blind before he came. Can you believe I cleaned up my entire apartment?"

"Was this your annual spring cleaning?"

"Julio, can you please stay with me here?"

35

"Who is 'he' anyway? And was 'he' a hundred percent blind?"

"Stop it. You know I'm talking about Bob, my mobility specialist. He never let on he was blind when he scheduled the appointment. And yes, he is one hundred percent blind."

"Do you always tell people you have a vision problem?"

I ignored his pointed question and huffed, "And why is it that blind people project their blindness onto others?"

"As if you are an expert on blind people now. Isn't he the first blind person that you ever met?" Julio scoffed. "You're in denial, big time."

"Oh shut up."

"So what was the end result of this all-important meeting?"

"I'm supposed to try out a cane for one session in my neighborhood. And get this—he wants me to wear dorky sleep shades," I grumbled. "Maybe he'll forget."

"Sleep shades. I like that. It'll be like you're sleepwalking. You're always lazing around in your bed, anyway."

"Julio, you're not helping."

"Wait. What do you mean you were *supposed* to try out a cane? Didn't you schedule it?"

With a cheeky grin, I said, "Nope, I have to call him when I have more time."

"I don't think that's smart," he said immediately. "What's the big deal about taking a walk in your own neighborhood?"

"You wouldn't understand. It's not you."

Of course, I never made the call.

However, my instructor kept on top of the situation. A few weeks later, I got a call. "Amy, Bob Braniff here, your mobility instructor."

As if I'd ever forget *that.*

"It's been awhile since we talked."

"Mm. Sorry, uh, so busy with my job lately."

"I know how that is," he commiserated. "But your cane has arrived now. Shall we take that trip in your neighborhood soon so you can try it out?"

He'd gone to a lot of trouble. I couldn't refuse. "Yeah, Bob. I can find time."

No more delays. We scheduled our session for mid-afternoon the next week in October.

Chapter 6
A New Kind of Sport

The big day arrived.

I heard a vehicle pull into the driveway. My mobility specialist. Already? Barefooted, I ran to meet him. "You're early, Bob."

"Take your time. I'll have a smoke." Bob got out of the van and took a pipe from the pocket of his jacket.

"Be right there."

I gathered my things together and returned. I didn't like to keep people waiting.

Pipe in hand, Bob stood outside the van talking to the driver. Once in awhile he lifted it to his lips and took a draw. The rich black cherry tobacco smoke that hung in the air brought back sweet memories of my father, another pipe smoker. I had a hunch Dad and Bob would have hit it off. No matter what their responsibilities, they both took time to shoot the breeze. Had they met, I'm sure they would have discovered mutual friends within their circles.

I stood up straight. Bob had emphasized good posture. "Ready."

I was really going to do this.

He snuffed out his pipe. "That's what I want to hear." He reached into his van and brought out a cellophane parcel. "Let me introduce you to your new cane."

Sorry to say this, Cane, but I'd rather not make your acquaintance.

Bob took off the wrap and unfolded each of the four sections so they fell into place and became one long cane. He produced a second, much smaller parcel sheathed in plastic wrap. "This contains your roller ball tip."

"It doesn't come with the cane?"

"No, the tip comes separately, which thus requires you to attach it before your first mobility training." He expertly pulled apart the plastic and extracted the tip. He guided my hand to the bottom of the cane. "It goes on here. Do you want to hook it on?"

Focused, I took the white plastic hook at the top of the roller ball tip in my hand. But instead of hooking it, the elastic snapped back into the bottom casing of the cane, pinching my thumb.

"Ow-ow-ow," I groaned, shaking my thumb back and forth. It had already turned purple and was bleeding. I dropped the cane as I brought my thumb to my lips to stop the pain.

Bob bent down to pick it up. He gingerly brushed it off.

"Sorry about that." Did I break my brand new cane already?

"Not a problem. It's tricky to get your fingers in the right place. Are you all right?"

"Yeah, sure," I said with my thumb still between my teeth.

Bob pulled until the elastic surfaced from the casing of the cane. "Want to try again?"

"No, thanks." I backed away.

I thought it ironic he could expertly secure the tip on without a whit of sight while I, the one who could see, fumbled. He placed the cane in my right hand. After a quick reminder of how to grip it, he instructed me to go ahead. "Just get a feel for it now."

We took to the sidewalk in front of my house with me in the lead. Shouldn't I be behind observing his good cane techniques? Probably not. I was the one who knew the area.

"Try walking with your eyes closed," Bob called.

Hey, what had happened to the sleep shades? Boy, was I glad he didn't bring them.

"Okay." I pretended, but didn't actually close my eyes.

I must have slowed down because I felt Bob's cane nick my heel. Time to speed up. "Bob, we're going to turn a corner here on Templeton Street."

"Templeton. A good solid name for a street."

The sun caressed my shoulders as I turned. Scattered dry leaves crunched at my feet as I moved along. The leaves caught under the tip of my cane as I swept it back and forth. It wasn't clear why I was sweeping it from side to side except that Bob instructed me to do so. If I had my way, I'd aim my cane like a pool cue and shoot a ball of leaves into life-sized pockets low on the ground. Yellow and orange ball in the corner pocket. Everyone would be amazed when they saw that I'd made such a tough shot.

Just then I jabbed myself hard in the stomach with my cane, and yelped. "Ack!"

The billiards game turned into a dagger of a fencing sport. "Ahh! Where's my shield?" I said loudly, massaging the area I poked. I silently bemoaned the fact I was not a knight living back in Shakespearean times and thus not properly armored.

"Speaking of where to yield, let me show you how to cross the street."

Oh, Bob misunderstood. I'd better stop daydreaming and pay attention. I'm in the middle of a lesson.

One of the things he pointed out was to always cross at a traffic light. For our practice, I took him around the corner to a busier road. "Okay, here it is."

"When you hold your cane vertically, it indicates to drivers that you are stopped and do not intend to cross the street. That's important. You then listen for sounds of traffic and yield the right-of-way to them if you hear vehicles in front of you. If you hear nothing, then you proceed to cross."

"This is Rice Avenue. There's the school where I teach mornings," I pointed out to Bob. What was I saying? He couldn't see any school.

If Bob thought anything strange about me pointing out a school he couldn't see, he never let on. But he jumped on the opportunity to promote more cane instruction. "That's the high school where you teach Spanish? I often conduct mobility training at the workplace. Would you like that?"

"It's a little part-time job," I said, as if I barely stepped in the building. "I get along pretty well there. I go straight from my classroom to the parking lot."

And what about the day the photographer came to take class pictures? Okay, so what if I stumbled down a couple of steps in an area I didn't know well. That could happen to anyone.

"Well, it's always helpful to familiarize yourself with other parts of the building. I can assist in that navigation." Bob had an eerie knack for looking past all the fluff without my saying a word.

We walked in silence for a few blocks. It didn't seem all that difficult. Except for a few cars, Bob and I had the street to ourselves. "This cane stuff isn't so bad."

I soon changed my tune. When I saw one of my neighbors, I intuitively longed to tuck my cane out of sight. *Why oh why did he have to be outside?* Oh no. I looked like I was cross-country skiing, except I had only one ski pole, and there wasn't any snow.

Soon we would pass him. He was dragging a lawn bag full of leaves to the curb. What would he think when he saw me with this weird stick? Of course he'd recognize me. We lived kitty-corner from each other.

I imagined what I'd say when we came face-to-face. I would stop, hold my cane vertically as if I were going to cross the street, except I'd turn and face my neighbor. What would I do? Twirl my cane like a drum majorette's baton? Or would I use it as a musician's lead and conduct a silent symphony, of course, introducing Bob as the master conductor? Better yet, I'd use my cane as a teacher's pointer and gesture dramatically at him. I would say, "As you can clearly see, I am now learning how to be blind." That would give him something to talk about.

When we came to his house, I did none of these things, of course. I felt my face heat up. What could I do? I waved at him and smiled.

Somehow Bob knew someone else was outdoors. "Nice day to be out and about, wouldn't you say?" Bob asked in his booming voice.

No response. My longtime neighbor stared as if he expected one of us to explain what was going on.

It wasn't going to be me. I closed my eyes for real. *No time like the present to try my skills.*

We arrived back at the house, and I led the way up the stairs to my sofa for our debriefing.

"You moved at a good clip," Bob said approvingly. Then his voice changed, and he almost seemed to be teasing me. "Especially toward the end."

"What do you mean?"

"Oh, like when we passed the gentleman not far from your house. You speeded up as soon as we left."

"You mean my neighbor? How did you know I speeded up?"

"Is that who it was? I wondered." He laughed then, a real belly laugh, which warmed up the room. "I could tell because your voice sounded a little bit fainter."

How amazing! Such a tiny detail and he noticed that.

All in all, the training went better than I thought it would. I felt good about my effort, and best of all, I learned a few things—even if I didn't like the stigma of using a cane.

"So how about our next mobility training? Your school will work well for the location."

"School's in session all day." Maybe that sounded defensive. But I wasn't totally on board with my mobility instructor invading my workspace.

He stroked his chin. "Quite understandable. How about if I come after classes finish, say three o'clock?"

"I'd have to ask the principal," I hedged, "She might have some kind of rule against that."

He lifted his cell phone to his ear, input some numbers, listened again, and turned to me with a confident expression on his face. "Yes, November fifteenth at three. Does that work for you?"

"What?" Did he just check his phone as if it were a calendar? "Umm...."

"Let's say, barring any rule the principal might have against bearded strangers, we'll meet up then."

"Bearded strangers? You don't have a beard."

"I will by then."

Chapter 7
Cane Training at the Academy

Bob and I bypassed the front door and entered the academy through the less-used teacher's door. I whispered, "Okay, this way." When I saw the coast was clear, I spoke in a normal tone. "All visitors have to sign in at the front office."

I peeked in the principal's office. She was tending to paperwork, as usual.

Mrs. Curtis, the only one I knew who rivaled Bob in height, stood up, extending a slender freckled arm. "It's my privilege to meet you, Mr. Braniff. Do whatever you need to do to make Amy more comfortable here."

"I certainly will." He looked at ease with his cane, not all stiff and formal like me. "Call me Bob," he said, removing his wool cap. When I saw him smooth his beard, I smiled. Neatly trimmed, it looked nice on him.

She beamed at me. "Take good care of Amy. She's our Spanish expert, and we need her."

I blushed at the compliment. She had a kind word for everyone.

Bob responded quickly and in all seriousness, "Fear not. Amy will be perfectly safe as she explores more of her work environment."

We got right to work. He asked me which areas of the school I frequented

44

and where I used my cane.

"Not in the classroom." I shuddered. "The students would see me."

"And why would that be a problem?"

Because they would *see* me. "Um, I know the layout of my room," I countered.

"So you have no problems in that environment?"

"No, I'm fine there."

"How about I take a look?" Bob said, lifting an eyebrow. "Perhaps I can identify areas that can be improved. By the way, you're still getting accustomed to handling the cane, so I will not introduce the sleep shades yet."

"All right." I pushed the door shut, and we began.

A little while later, Bob pointed out that someone was knocking at the door. How could he hear it and not me? Even with my hearing aids, I didn't catch everything. I opened the door, and there stood one of my colleagues.

They exchanged greetings while I politely waited.

All smiles, Bob added by way of explanation, "I'm encouraging Amy to use her cane in the classroom—as well as in the rest of the school—to develop that extra measure of confidence."

Bob! Stop! I wanted to shout. It was none of her business. She'd never seen me with a cane—up until now. Why couldn't we do this in an area where there weren't any other teachers? I wasn't ready to "share" this part of myself yet.

The teacher gathered some Bibles from the bookshelf and a handful of folders from the filing cabinet along with a stack of papers. "That's very good of you. I'm sure it will serve her well."

Why were they talking as if I wasn't here? This wasn't a parent-teacher conference. It was as if Bob had joined forces with the teacher and together, they planned to coax me into better behavior. I stiffened, my cane still in my hand. My cheeks flamed as I listened to them.

Did he really think that using my cane would bring *extra* confidence? All my students would think about was that darned cane and not the lesson at hand.

The instructor opened the top drawer of the filing cabinet. "Do you mind if I stay for a couple of minutes? I have a few papers to file."

Bob jumped in with a response before I could even get a word out. "It's certainly not a problem for me. It depends on how comfortable Amy feels with another person in the room." He turned to me. "Are you all right with it?"

I wasn't "all right" with her staying. If only I could be honest. I should have guessed Bob would put all the pressure on me to decide. How could I embarrass the instructor? Besides, the academy used this classroom for Spanish, Bible, and Art classes. It wasn't my private space, after all. "I'm fine," I lied. I kept up appearances and made sure to smile and comment at the appropriate times since her arrival had turned into an impromptu chat session.

"I believe the time has come to negotiate the stairs," Bob said after a bit.

My colleague slipped a paper into a manila file and said casually, "If you go through the accountant's office, you'll find some stairs. Or there are some stairs leading to the cafeteria."

"Perfect!" Bob enthused, "Which would you prefer?"

"I don't know." Neither.

"Do you know where that office is, Amy?"

"Kind of. I can probably find it." Mrs. Dresser's office was right outside the copy room. I knew exactly how to get there.

When we arrived, I let Bob take the lead and explain our goals.

Mrs. Dresser, the accountant, nodded throughout the explanation. She looked stricken. "By all means," she said softly. "Let me show you the way."

I tried to smile, pretending I was fine with my cane and it was just another day in my life. Bob was damaging my reputation here with my colleagues. Did he realize that?

Oh boy. That look on Mrs. Dresser's face let me know that a light bulb had gone off in her head. Now last week's accident made sense. I had walked smack into a thick cement column in the lobby and almost knocked myself out as I left school from the front entrance, one I rarely used. Hearing the commotion, Mrs. Dresser had run to my side. Sprawled on the floor and somewhat dazed, I must have been a frightening sight.

"Let me get some ice for your head!" She had scurried away and returned quickly, carrying a baggie with ice. "You're bleeding," she observed. "Keep the ice on that cut."

Sheepishly, I had doled out my usual explanation, that I was accident prone.

"These things happen. I hope you're getting enough sleep," she worried.

She had led me into the nurse's office, a tiny side room containing only a cot and no nurse. (Our faculty members wore many hats.) She had insisted I lie down until my ride arrived.

Now that she knew why the accident happened, I prayed she wouldn't bring it up to my mobility instructor. He didn't need any more ammunition against me.

"Here are the stairs," Mrs. Dresser said, leading us to the top step. There, her hand hovered over the light switch. "Shall I turn on the light?"

"No," Bob said, firmly. "The best environment is darkness, so Amy can learn how to navigate by using non-visual techniques."

"If you need anything, give me a shout," she said, and went back to her money figures.

I was glad to have the scant light coming from her office to illuminate part of the first step. Thank God, my instructor couldn't see it. He'd made it clear I shouldn't be relying so much on my sight in these practice sessions. Bob showed me how to measure the depth of the step by holding my cane vertically. Then he dropped the tip of the cane straight down. "That's how you find the next step."

Mastering this technique required natural rhythm. If I went too fast, I'd overstep my cane. If I went too slowly, I'd lose track of the next step. I made my way down, counting each one silently. Five. *Clunk-step.* Six. *Clunk-step.* Se...Clunk-*no step!* The abrupt change interrupted my momentum and threw me off balance. "Oh, I didn't know I'd reached the bottom! How did I lose count?"

"You don't need to count. Just let your cane drop first. It will alert you to the next step."

I was getting tired. My response, a grunt, must have conveyed my fatigue because he changed tactics. "What is the darkest room in this school?"

"I guess the sanctuary." Please, let's just finish.

"It would be helpful for you to have some mobility practice in a larger space. Are you game?" He sounded eager.

I took a deep breath. "Right, okay."

We had to turn around and climb the stairs. I tried to remember his instructions but everything I was learning ran together so I climbed them any old way. Thank God, he didn't insist on "the right technique."

We arrived at the sanctuary, a feat that surprised me since I'd only been there once before. Shivering in the unheated and pitch black room, I didn't have any choice but to rely on my cane. Bob and I each explored the space on our own. Without supervision or fear of doing it wrong, I became more adventurous. My cane found a long pew. I followed that out until my cane touched only carpet again, then I changed directions and tapped my cane against ... something hard. A few more taps told me what I needed to know. A table! I continued tapping ... wood! Oh yeah, I'm getting good at this. I set out to discover my next target ... a step. I slid my cane over it and felt the texture. Carpeting.

It wasn't until our two canes clashed that I remembered Bob. I giggled nervously, pulling my cane back, feeling like I'd overstepped my bounds and invaded his personal space.

"Shall we return to your teaching quarters and prepare for our departure?"

"Yes, we shall," I said, as if he'd asked me to step out on a Victorian dance floor.

A quick glance at the clock in my classroom showed it was after four o'clock. Our session had gone past the hour.

As we retraced our steps to the teacher's entrance, several sounds caught my attention—feet running, some shouting, a shrill whistle and the dribbling of a ball. "It's the gym." My voice squeaked. "They're having girls' basketball practice. Let's get out of here!"

My stomach churned, and I turned away—but not quickly enough. Coming down the steps from the opposite direction were two girls from my Spanish class who played on the team. They must have been in the bathroom.

The taller of the two greeted me, "*Hola, profesora.*"

How do I explain this?

As usual, Bob butted in before I had the chance to think it through. "Hello, young lady. Ms. Bovaird is giving me a tour of your excellent facility with our canes."

I couldn't believe my ears. How could Bob do this to me? My teaching career was ruined! I could see it now. My Spanish students would blab it to other students—starting with girls on the team—that I was walking around the school with a blind man. They'd whisper, "You won't believe it but *Profesora* Bovaird was also using one of those sticks." They'd looked shocked and say, "No way. Do you think she's blind, too?"

Without knowing what to do or say, I simply stood awkwardly, my hand gripping my cane, my face flushed, my heart racing. *Now* how would I get out of the situation?

The girls came to the rescue. "We need to get back to our practice." After a chorus of "see-you-laters," the girls waved goodbye and left.

"Lord, how could today be any worse?" I mumbled. "Get me out of here!" In a louder voice, I guided Bob to the door. "Straight ahead and push."

Finally back in the parking lot, I let out a big sigh. It was *such* a relief to simply follow my mobility specialist and leave the navigating to him. I don't know how he knew where to go but he always got where he needed to be. I couldn't wait to get in the van and go home. What color was it? It didn't matter. Bob would know.

Maybe he recognized the particular sound of the motor, or perhaps the horn. My guess would be it was his super-duper, finely-tuned hearing abilities. Whatever the manner, Bob was meticulous. Whether he used his fail-free cardinal coordinates—north, south, east and west—or let his cane find the way, soon I'd be home and this terrible afternoon would end.

Since Bob had such long legs, he covered a lot of ground quickly. I didn't even have time to fold up my cane. I rushed after him, half-heartedly sweeping it as I went. Would I ever be as confident as Bob with a cane? I noticed that his height gave him an added air of importance. People looked up to him when they shook his hand. And his voice, it could be heard in the next state over! I believe that people remembered those aspects of him more than the fact he was blind.

On the other side of the parking lot, I glimpsed a van. Bob must have heard it with his sonar hearing or had pre-planned to meet the driver on that side of the parking lot because he turned in the direction of the van. Without hesitation, he pulled the door open and stepped through the passenger's door.

A few feet behind Bob, I reached for the handle and slid the side door open. I nearly stepped into the vehicle. One look at the driver and I backed away.

The mother of one of my students recognized me. She looked startled at the unfamiliar man with a beard getting into her car. Her eyes traveled to his cane and back to mine. "Excuse me..." she said.

He smiled and waved goodbye as he backed out again. He did not seem embarrassed nor was he apologetic. Bob soon found the correct vehicle and eased himself into the front passenger's seat.

I wish I were as calm. All I could think of was that now even the parents would know.

The parking lot was filled with high school students. The one thing I'd learned about teenagers over the past few months, they loved their social media. It was the end of the day so they could use their cell phones. I imagined my photo all over Facebook, Twitter, and whatever other social media sites I hadn't yet heard of. Maybe I'd even make the 5:00 news.

This gave new meaning to the blind leading the blind.

Julio called me to get the scoop on my mobility training. When I shared the awful stories, he laughed.

"This is not funny!" Why did life have to be so difficult? Having a bruised ego and then having someone laugh on top of that made me want to scream. "I have to find a new job. It's only a matter of time before I lose control in the classroom." A monotone female voice rattled off something in the background. It took a few seconds for it to register what I was hearing—his GPS. "Are you driving?"

"Yeah, why? I'm on speaker phone."

"Figures. You're going to be distracted now."

"You must be talking about yourself? I'm the multi-tasker, remember?"

I rolled my eyes.

"What's the problem with people finding out? That opens the door for discussion. It's the perfect opportunity for you to take in your cane and *show* it," he said, as if explaining all this to a very slow learner.

"I can't do that."

He sounded exasperated. "Why not?"

"I. Can't. Do. That."

"Yes, you can. You know, pretend that it's Show and Tell. Whatever. You're a teacher. Do what teachers do—teach."

Beep-beep-beep-beep-beep. "What's that noise?"

"I'm backing up and parking here at the print shop. I need to go now. You're going to tell them, aren't you? I don't want to have to write your lesson plans for you. Or call your principal. Believe me, the students will be a lot nicer when they discover why you're tripping over desks and walking into walls. I'll give you a call later."

"Hmmph." I switched off my phone. A good nap seemed in order. "He's right. It's no big deal. I'll show them my cane tomorrow. I'll do it for sure."

The next morning, determined to address the situation, I walked into class with my cane and set it on the table. Moments before the students arrived, I picked it up and hid it in the filing cabinet. I didn't take it out again.

Chapter 8
RUNNING AWAY

Mom handed me the mail. She tapped the top envelope with a slender arthritic finger. "This looks like what you've been waiting for—your pay from the college. Open it up."

That's what I love about my mom. When good things happen to me, she gets as excited as if they happened to her.

"You're right, dadadaDUH!" I did a little dance. "No more Asian Studies class. No more lectures or exams to prepare. No more shrieking students." Freedom!

Mom jabbed me in the side. "You'll have to share some of that mooh-lah with your mother."

"You're right. Reese's Cups on the house."

Now I only had my high school students to worry about. If any of the students at the academy heard about "the episode," as I referred to Bob and my fiasco, they never let on. Because I only taught a few classes, I didn't interact with much of the faculty or staff. When I did, however, it became clear they knew about my vision problems.

One morning at work, a note in my pigeonhole instructed me to stop in the accountant's office. She needed information to reimburse me for some out-of-pocket expenses for class material.

The niggling in my stomach made me head toward my classroom instead.

Right before class finished, Mrs. Curtis popped through my door. "Don't forget to see Mrs. Dresser before you leave today, so we can get your money back to you." She gave a cheerful smile. My principal liked efficiency.

"Yeah, sure. Thanks."

The bell rang, and my students filed out of class.

I'd better get this out of the way.

"Mornin', I got your note. You needed some information?" I said with a breeziness I didn't feel.

After we finished business, she touched my shoulder gently. "How did your practice session go with the gentleman I saw you with?"

"Fine." I didn't want to talk about it. I smiled tightly and backed away. "Thank you so much for asking. Sorry, I have to run. My um, my brother's waiting."

Outside the door on my way out to my brother, it was just my luck that I ran into a parent of one of my students. She saw my cane but didn't seem surprised. "Amy, I'm so sorry. How do you manage? I had no idea…."

Was that pity in her voice?

Pity. The one thing I can't stand. I'm as capable as any one of the teachers here. I dare anyone to say my students are not progressing in their language skills!

That afternoon, I bundled up and went for a long run. Despite the cold, when my feet hit the pavement, I felt in control—at least in this one area. *My life is a mess*, I complained to God. If only I knew someone, anyone else going through what I was, it would be easier. Should I be angry? Touched? How could I handle all the emotions going through my head? *Father, I know that this parent has a good heart. And all the teachers and staff at the school are kind and caring. But I don't want anyone to treat me differently.*

I let my thoughts flow as I continued to run, recalling an incident a week earlier.

I'd asked Mrs. Curtis if I could show a video to my Spanish III student. She paused, as was her custom, to think through my request. "I see no problem as long as it ties into the goals for your student."

"Yes, of course. It's a DVD of *Fuenteovejuna,* the literature we're reading now. I can't wait for her to see it. You know, it's by the sixteenth century playwright, *Lope de Vega.* Did you know his play is based on actual events during an uprising in Spain?"

Her eyes had crinkled at the corners as she shared my enthusiasm. "Is that right?"

"Yes, it's all in Spanish. Maybe a little difficult for her to follow—they're native speakers, after all—but I'll only show a couple of scenes, and she knows that part of the story." I saw the principal glance at the clock, so I got to the point. "I just need to know where the TV is."

"Why, it's right there in that old sanctuary not far from your classroom," she had said. She made a face. "That's right, you can't see the TV. Sorry, I forgot."

My jaw dropped. Of course I could see the TV. I'd just forgotten where it was.

If I weren't so hush-hush about this entire vision thing, others would have a much better idea of my abilities. They wouldn't have to guess the worst.

My run had turned into a slow jog. I could hear my labored breathing. *God, why am I so secretive? How can I change?*

I can do all things through Christ who strengthens me. No, if I talk about it, people will feel sorry for me. No one wants that.

Trust Me.

But God, it's so hard. I don't want anyone to know. I can't open up.

Look what happened already.

Another scripture jumped into my head. *What is impossible with men is possible with God.*

"Ow!" My foot hit an uneven edge of the sidewalk, and my ankle turned. I landed on the sidewalk, scraping first my right, then my left knee. My ankle hit hard, and I fell forward. I lay there for half a minute before I changed my position to sit and assess the damage. White hat, covered in mud. Ski jacket, torn in the sleeve. A tear in the right knee of my blue jeans. My knee tingled. I brushed off the gravel and pressed my hand against it to stop the sudden shaking. No blood this time. I turned to my ankle. Swollen. The tears came, hot and heavy as I doubled over. I hate my life! One minute I'm okay, the next minute, I can't even walk. Why? Why? Why me? Why is my life so complicated? I let myself cry for a few minutes.

No one has it easy. Look around and see how many are struggling. You have Me to guide you. I will never leave you or forsake you.

Even so, I continued to cry.

I stopped crying a few minutes later. Okay, God. Enough of this pity party. How can I blame others for feeling sorry for me if I give in and do the same thing? I gingerly stood up to see if I could put any pressure on my ankle and took a few limping steps.

A car drove up and the driver rolled down his window. "Are you okay?"

"Yes, yes, of course," I said, my old pride kicking in.

"Do you live nearby? Would you like a lift home?"

"No, no, no. I'm fine. Thank you so much."

"Sure?"

"Yep." I nodded several times to reassure him.

It was only when I tripped a second time, long after the man drove away, that I realized God had probably sent him to encourage me.

Why do I thwart You, God, at every turn? I continued slowly home. People should just call me Old Limp-along.

Chapter 9
COPING WITH STRESS

Over the next few months, Bob called me a couple of times. The only number he had was to our home phone. Mom, who usually answered, would hold it out to me. I'd shake my head and mouth the words, "Tell him I'm not home." She'd give an appropriate excuse but frown at me. "You need to talk to him. Tell him you're not interested. Don't make *me* lie to him."

"Sorry, Mom. I don't know what to do."

While I avoided Bob, other members of the Bureau of Blindness task force met with me. From the technician side, David provided me with a special large laptop. He ordered a program called *Zoomtext,* which changed the screen text and background in a number of ways to help vision-impaired people see it more easily.

Like Bob, David, too, was a hundred percent blind. I found his presence soothing—maybe because he didn't require anything of me. But also, he seldom used a cane. He preferred having a sighted guide, a close friend who came and left with him.

In the background, I heard the low but constant running commentary coming from JAWS, a special operating program for the blind, which spewed out continuous descriptive instruction, enabling him to format my laptop.

"David," I said, "Do you ever feel you have to tell people you're blind?"

He seemed to know I was grappling with this issue.

"Amy, that's entirely up to you. Do you have *any* sight?"

"Yes, I do. A lot." I wondered what he thought about that. If I had "a lot," what would I be doing with the Bureau of Blindness?

"Well, you only need to share what you want to." David felt behind the laptop, inserted a USB cable and slipped a CD in the machine. "Don't let anyone push you into saying or doing what you're not ready for."

"Yeah, that's right. I don't want to do that. Sometimes I do feel kind of pressured around certain people." Like Bob. *I'm not going to start announcing, "I'm blind!" when that's just not true.*

"We all struggle to some degree. But you need to feel at peace with who you are in whatever way that is for you. I'm a Native American and peaceful by nature. I don't let people rock me. I *am* the rock."

I watched his face as he spoke. He wasn't joking, and he didn't elaborate. "What do you mean?"

He paused. "You don't have to tell people. Right now, cultivate the positive in yourself and your situation."

"Oh." Me, a rock? No way. I crossed my arms. "It's more like I'm between a rock and a hard place," I said, my lips set in a tight line. "I don't need to tell anyone. My cane does it for me." I made a face. "You know that red part? I feel like I should charge through the crowd and yell, 'Fire engine coming through!' That's exactly what it's like."

He laughed—a pleasant, relaxed sound that eased the edges of the hard bitter pit that always seemed to exist in the center of my stomach. Then he turned toward me. "All you need is a siren."

"Woo-woo-woo. Move over. Out of the way." I imagined people racing to either side of the walkway as I barreled through with my horrid cane.

"Ha! Your siren sounds more like one in a cop car."

I let out a long dramatic sigh. "Details, details."

"Plug this in, will you?" He handed me the cord to the laptop. "Bet you really book down the sidewalk, too, huh?"

"I do, actually. Why do you say that?"

He concentrated on the task at hand then said, "Well, it only stands to reason. You speak fast, don't you?"

"Yeah, that's true." I laughed. "Woo-woo-woo. Fire engine comin' through."

He cupped his hands to his mouth. "Where's the fire? It better not be anywhere near me." He patted down his clothes in mock fear.

"Or my brand new laptop." I laughed "I'm sure the State would frown on that."

The cane I rarely used suddenly caught my eye. It hung, all bright and shiny, on its nail in the kitchen. I noticed the final section with its fire-engine-red color immediately preceding the tip. It took up less than a foot of the cane.

"Hey, David," I said, feeling more at ease than I had in awhile. "You almost done?"

It made all the difference in my outlook that I didn't *have* to tell people. I had a choice. Maybe I *could* be a rock.

Chapter 10
Opening My Mind

The Bureau of Blindness also sent Francis, a life skills teacher, to help me problem-solve any difficulty I might have relating to home living. Unlike Bob and David, Fran could see fine and visited me once a month. At first, she arrived with all her lists. Did I need a special cutting board to keep all the vegetables from falling onto the floor? How about a placard for the family car that would allow me to park in a handicapped zone? What about lights? Could I use stronger lights? Did I need bright-colored water-resistant tape to mark the edges of my countertop? Would I like to enroll in the Hadley School for the Blind? Get free audio books? Did I need a machine that announced the colors of my clothing? Fran held it up to my shirt. A toneless, electronic voice read 'Blue.' "It can even detect patterns, like stripes or plaid," she said, grinning.

"Really? Then I should have worn polka dots just to test if the machine would pick it up."

"It's pretty handy," she said, placing it back in her bag.

I answered "Yes," to most things, though I thought hard about the handicapped space but finally decided that Mom could benefit from a placard. *I* certainly had no problem walking any distance. I also turned down the machine that detected color. As much as I admired it, someone else could benefit more from it. I could still match my own clothing—most of the time. I didn't want to waste the government's money on something I didn't need.

Fran also offered to teach me Braille. As a foreign language teacher, this intrigued me. Would learning Braille turn out to be like learning any other foreign language?

"Yes, that'll be great. Bring me the manual!"

Fran's eyes widened, and she laughed. "That's not a response I often hear. I'm thrilled you're willing to learn it. Although it takes quite a long time to become proficient in Braille, it's well worth the effort." She jotted something down on her list.

The dog came to the sofa where we sat and barked. "He's letting us know that we're sitting on his bed," I said. "Shhh, Buddy. Lay down."

"Oh." She didn't seem to be a dog person. Still focused on her task, she continued. "There are actually two books. Book One features introductory material such as the alphabet, short practice words and phrases and takes you to the sentence level. This is called uncontracted Braille, or Braille in its simplest form."

"Right. Pretty much like any beginner's language textbook." I could deal with that.

She smoothed the cushion on my sofa. "Book Two features contracted Braille."

"You mean words like he's, they're, it's, couldn't, didn't, those kinds of words, right?"

"You'd think, huh? No, contracted Braille uses a combination of raised dots for one word instead of one letter at a time."

"Really? I like that."

Once the books came in, I wondered how on earth I'd ever learn. I couldn't see the dots. Though I knew the point was to *feel* them, the white pages still seemed overwhelming. "I'll practice. I know I can do it. I'm good at languages," I assured her.

We worked half an hour that day. I liked it so much more than learning to thread a needle blindfolded. But after several tries and various methods, I even accomplished that. I laughed about it later with my mom. "I don't even sew buttons on now. When will I ever sew a button on when I'm blind?"

I didn't realize I'd said that so naturally—*when I'm blind*. These visits had opened my eyes to new possibilities.

Thoughts of mobility training and Bob crept back into my days. I committed the situation to prayer.

God, do you think I'm being close-minded? I'm always frustrated and worried about how people are going to respond to me. Have I distorted my fears? All my friends tell me this mobility training will help me and make life easier. But how do they know? They're not losing their vision. They don't have to face the stares. The stares I'm not supposed to see. They don't have to be labeled as "different." I'm so tired of trying to figure out what to do. Lord, show me.

A few nights after that prayer, I listened to a song called *God Use Me* by Andy Landis, a Christian country-western singer. This song had meant a lot to me several years earlier at another difficult time in my life. Suddenly, it spoke to me again.

In the song, the woman talks to God. She begs Him to listen to her and shares how she's grateful for all the things He's done in her. I could imagine the bowed head and her contrite heart. She acknowledges that He has a plan and always finishes what He starts, comparing His faithfulness in fulfilling it to the flow of the river. Her voice becomes more yielding as she sings about how she hears Him calling deep within her heart. I could feel a stirring renew in my own. Her words became my words. She sings how though she's far from what she should be, she wants to serve Him faithfully and asks God to use her for a higher purpose.

It was the last couple of lines that really jumped out at me. The singer lowered her voice and sang them with a heartfelt realization. Everything she had was *His*. I could feel the surrender as she whispered for Him to use her to impact others.

It became my surrender.

Heavenly Father, is this Your answer? Even my sight belongs to You. It's not mine to pick and choose what to do with it. You do always finish what You start. I don't. I didn't finish my mobility training. My fears got the best of me. God, how can You use someone who's losing her vision to show Your love? I'm so imperfect—such a baby sometimes. But You can use me—if I trust You with my fears. You have a purpose in my vision loss. Shape me into what You will.

You're so patient with me. You sent me someone who hasn't given up on me. Bob wants the best for me. He doesn't have to keep calling me. He gets paid whether I take the training or not. God, I've been selfish—not listening and refusing to see Your will for my life. You want only to make my life easier. The answer to my prayer has been here all along, only it wasn't packaged in the way I expected.

You sent the absolute best person, someone who knows what I'm facing. A smart, clever man, someone who can bounce back after sitting on my dog and even after getting in the wrong van. Even if he's not losing his vision, he knows what it's like not to have any vision. Of course, You're providing for me now, just like You've done any other time in my life.

God, how could I have been so blind?

The tears that came next were those of relief as I finally gave my burden to God. I knew it would take daily surrender, but trusted that He would help me focus on the plan He had to better my life. And He would use me to encourage others who struggled—maybe with vision loss. Maybe simply with living.

The next day after work I called the Bureau of Blindness and Visual Services and asked for Bob.

Chapter 11
IT'S THE SAME WORLD

Though officially spring, it felt more like winter. With patches of snow dotting nearby yards and parts of driveways, it seemed a harsh start to my new resolve. Bob and I met in the back driveway. The driver watched in the car while Bob prepared me for our first "blind" walk.

He held several newly-purchased black eye masks in his hand. "The time has come to fit one of these sleep shades over your eyes. I have several, so you'll need to inform me which one you feel most comfortable with."

I slipped the first one over my eyes. I hummed the theme to the 1956 Batman series. "To the batpole, Robin. I mean, Bob."

He paused, probably trying to figure out what I was talking about. "Here," he said handing over a much larger pair. "See what you think of these."

"I like these." The floppy sleep shades had soft cushioning all around the edges, which extended down the bridge for my nose and helped to keep them snug around my eyes.

"That's good. Try these and see how you like them," he said, offering a third one.

"Not good, not bad. I prefer the second pair," I declared, stretching the elastic behind my head and removing the one I wore. "Why do I need to wear these things again?"

"For you to benefit from your training, it's essential that you practice in the conditions when you most need your cane. The goal is to get you to stop relying on your sight. Wearing sleep shades forces you to apply the non-visual mobility techniques I'm teaching in order for you to get around better."

"Oh yeah, that's right."

"Don't worry, I'll wear one, too. So we'll both look somewhat peculiar."

Bob fussed with my mask, making sure it was tight enough. "Did you remember to bring your cane?"

"Yes. Got it." The raw, March air chilled me as I gripped the cane in one hand and held on to my hood, which was flapping in the wind, with the other. "I wish I'd brought my gloves."

"You'll warm up once we get moving," Bob assured me. "We need to leave from Lake Street, you said, so where is that located from where we are?"

"It's straight ahead."

Our route consisted of walking a quarter of a mile up the street in front of my house to a wooden footbridge I knew from childhood. Crossing over the bridge would put us in the next town. We'd walk to the end of that street, then turn around and retrace our steps.

My instructor put me in the lead and called out suggestions to guide me along.

I started out slowly, almost shuffling—tapping for the familiar. Where had all these stones come from? When did the sidewalk get so uneven? I knew the curb was somewhere, but where? Where? The tip of my cane tapped against a hard-curved surface. "We're at the corner, Bob."

"Okay, listen for cars," Bob instructed. We waited for a couple of minutes. "There isn't much traffic here, is there? Okay, let's cross."

On the other side, I headed west—at least I hoped it was west.

"Stay on the sidewalk. Sweep your cane back and forth to find the hard surface. Feel that?"

"Yeah," I said, breathless.

"If you feel something soft, you've wandered onto someone's lawn. Just take nice smooth sweeping movements and go forward at a steady pace. That's it. Excellent!"

"How do you know, Bob?"

"I can hear the way your cane is moving and where your voice is coming from."

Wow. It's true. When one sense is taken, the others become more acute. That was so cool. Would mine get stronger, too? No. I was losing my hearing. For just a second, I actually forgot about that.

"Keep going. You're doing great!" Bob continued.

Or I was until I heard a vehicle move. Up close. Loud. *Beep-beep-beep.* Is that driver backing up? I listened. Didn't move a millimeter. Couldn't.

"You aren't in any danger, Amy. Keep going."

Where was that vehicle? What if the driver didn't see me? What if I walked into its path? What if he backed over me?

I could hear the screech of brakes, the scrape of the something heavy being lifted, indistinct mumbling, running, more movement. The sounds began to fade.

"You were fine," Bob reassured me, "Is today garbage day in your neighborhood? It sounded very much like two able-bodied males loading a heavy truck again and again. It stopped next to you, not in front of or behind you."

My breath came in short pants, like Buddy's did after a long run. It's okay, I told myself sternly. I'm all right. I took a deep breath and forced myself to continue.

"That's it. Take your cane out farther."

A train whistle startled me. "The train tracks must be ahead, just under the bridge we'll be walking on."

It took five minutes before my cane found the wooden slats. "We've made it to the footbridge!" I shouted.

"Keep going."

We had just crossed to the other side of the bridge when a succession of powerful rumbles and hissing sounds came to my attention. I strained to hear. What *is* that? "Oh! That must be the school busses leaving to pick up the kids."

"There's a grammar school nearby?"

"Yeah. I hope we don't get caught up in the school traffic. We'd better head back." I turned and surged forward as if I could see.

"Amy. Whoa! Come back." Bob's voice sounded serious but not alarmed.

Where am I? I froze at the sound of a vehicle v-e-r-y close.

Again, I heard Bob's voice, slow and steady. "You've wandered across the road. Come back."

Gladly. Just tell me where to "come back" to. How did Bob know that I'd wandered across the road? I simply trusted that he did. Then, in a flash of nervous energy, I gripped my cane and swung in a series of arcs around me, spinning in a small tight circle. "Bob, where are you? I can't see."

"Stay put. Listen to my voice. Do you hear more traffic?"

"Yes-s-s." But from which side?

My muscles were tightly coiled, ready to spring into action but I didn't know where to go.

"Put your cane straight up and down. Remember? That will tell the driver you are not going to cross the street. Do that *now*."

I immediately responded.

The vroom of the engine drowned out any other thought I might have had at that moment.

With the immediate danger over, I let out a breath. "Where am I, Bob?"

"The opposite side of the road. Just cross over again. Listen to my voice. Come here."

I listened intently, trying to pinpoint Bob's voice and began to cross with steady sweeping movements like he taught me to make. His voice grew closer. My cane swept back and forth until I hit a hard surface. The sidewalk? I swept a few more times and tapped the soft surface on each side to be sure. Yes, the sidewalk. Back to safety!

"See? You made it."

"Yippee!" I wanted to rip the sleep shades off my eyes then and there. A mixture of laughter, excitement, and adrenalin surged through me. "Can I take my sleep shades off now?"

"Not quite yet."

I groaned, but continued on.

Finally, I said, "We should be nearing my house by now. Can I peek?"

After a long pause, Bob said, "Yes, I give you permission to remove your sleep shades."

I yanked at the elastic, and the sleep shades flew off. Hallelujah! It took a few minutes for my eyes to adjust to the light. Then I noticed something incredible. "My house is the next one over. Can you believe it? Hey, Bob, we did it!"

"Of course we did."

Though I had known this street my entire life, that afternoon I learned how unfamiliar even an area I knew so well could be without sight. My companion was blind. Yet I had asked him questions as if he could see the layout of every street and obstacle. He had existed in my world, and I in his. With our roles reversed, I felt the barriers between us fall away.

"I can't believe I did that!" I bubbled over. "When I put on my blindfold I experienced your world the whole time."

"They're *sleep shades*, not blindfolds."

I didn't have to ask what the difference was. Bob let me know.

"You're blindfolded when you play children's games. Sleep shades simulate the conditions in which you will one day find yourself. Don't forget that," he said sternly. "By the way, we all live in *one* world, although we may respond to this world through different senses. I am teaching you how to respond non-visually."

"I never thought of it from that perspective," I said, slowly.

"You wouldn't have, without this training. Up until this point, you've experienced life with your physical vision. Now you're coming to understand that this world can be met visually, at those times when you can see, and non-visually, for those times when you can't. The non-visual techniques are no less legitimate than visual techniques, and they are no less safe."

So much information to digest!

"Bob, thanks for watching my back." I grinned at the paradox of my words. Yet, that's exactly what he had done.

My sleep shades had taught me the value of developing my skills. No more blindfolds.

Back in my apartment when Bob and I had our debriefing, he noted my excitement. "You're really happy about today's training, aren't you?"

"Of course." I rubbed my hands together and repeated Bob's earlier words, "It's the *same* world. Bob, wow!" An ecstatic sigh escaped me. "God used you to teach me a life-changing lesson today."

A frown came to his face, and he looked away. Then he turned back to me, composed. "You're easy to teach, and optimistic," he said, ignoring my mention of God.

I smiled. "Believe me, that's not all me. It's God working through my situation."

"God. Hmm." I saw a brooding expression come over Bob's face. "I had a close friend, an old woman who served God as much as she could. She suffered terribly…." Suddenly, his eyes narrowed. "Tell me why God would let someone that dedicated die!"

"Bob, sometimes, it's…we don't know why. But, your friend isn't in pain any longer," I said softly.

"No thanks to the all-powerful God," he scoffed, his jaw set obstinately. "I, we, *needed* her." Bob clenched his hands and sat motionless.

My heart went out to him, instinctively knowing Bob was struggling to deal with his loss. Later, it occurred to me that while Bob shared his mobility lessons with me, perhaps I had something to share with him, too.

Lord, I don't know what exactly to say, so please comfort Bob in the way only You can.

"Julio, I could do it! The garbage truck was so scary, but Bob knew what it was, and I was on the wrong side of the road and everything!"

"Slow down," he said, exasperated. "How did you know where you were if you were wearing sleep shades?"

"Bob told me."

"Right. A blind man told you that you were on the wrong side of the road," he repeated skeptically.

"That's right. He's amazing! He studied how to teach, you know. I trust him more now."

"Is this the same Ms. I-Can't-Do-That speaking?"

"Humph. That's a different subject."

The next morning I stopped by Mrs. Curtis's office and shared the whole story of my training with her.

"What an answer to prayer!" she exclaimed. "I've been praying for you."

"Really?" It was so easy to talk to her. She encouraged me at every turn.

"Yes. You are making such progress," she noted, clapping her hands gently.

I liked her long slender hands; they were hands that served. She dished out cafeteria food with those hands. She'd also served food she'd made at the faculty brunch with those same hands. She'd vacuumed the halls and picked up paper wads students left behind. She had a servant's hands and a servant's heart.

"You know, Mrs. Curtis, it seems like there are two worlds out there, one for the blind and one for the sighted. But it's actually the same world. Although people's frame of reference might be different, we interact with the same variables. That's what Bob told me."

"Well said." She nodded understandingly. "I'm glad you're feeling better about your training."

"For years I feared losing my vision because I couldn't imagine how I'd cope in a blind world. Then God brought Bob. Now Bob's showing me that I can do it. It's a tiny step in faith. It's still so scary, but maybe, maybe, not quite as much as before."

Mrs. Curtis put on her principal's hat again. "Would you be willing to speak to the high school students at chapel one day? They need the exposure to positive role models stepping out in faith."

I backed away. "Oh no, I couldn't ever do that!"

"It's okay. Just pray about it. You might change your mind," she soothed. "If the Holy Spirit leads you, maybe we can shoot for the end of the year."

Forget that. There was no way I'd be talking to those students.

CHAPTER 12
AIMING FOR A 20/20 ATTITUDE

Shortly after the mobility training and before my next Braille lesson, I had an appointment with Doc Pritchard. I took a field of vision test to measure the extent of my useful vision. Doc also promised me he'd put together some fancy gadgets to help me see a little better. "Hey, I'll try whatever you have," I told him.

A week later, I received a call back from Doc Pritchard.

"Well, I have good news and bad news. Which do you want to hear first?" The words hung in the air between my droll ophthalmologist and me. I paused—long enough for the phone to crackle.

"Doc, tell me the bad news first so the good news sounds better."

"The *bad* news is that … I am not getting any younger." He coughed as if he knew the joke wouldn't fare well at Comedy Central.

This comedian needed to perfect his comic timing or refine his jokes.

"Now the *good* news is that while your vision is not going to win any awards, you have the best vision of any RP patient in your age group that I've ever seen. Your nerve is still in good shape. It's not yellowed or cracked. As I said, best I've seen. And you've already lived—what? More than half your life.

How many years you got left? Chances are, you may even retain some vision 'til the end."

I could feel the corners of my mouth turning upward as the eye doctor blundered on, trying to cushion the blow in his odd-humored way. Who could deny his good intentions?

"So what *is* my field of vision exactly, Doc?"

"Come into the office, and we'll talk numbers. Keep in mind, numbers are just that. They don't mean much," he muttered.

The day of my appointment arrived. I slipped off my gloves and blew on my fingers to warm them, then removed my hat and scarf and took a seat, folding up my cane. We were either having a late winter or a lousy spring.

In his office, Doc sat down with me and explained my situation.

"We're gonna' talk degrees here. You already know that your left eye is bad. It has about five degrees, and the right eye, which is better, has about eight degrees."

I nodded. "So, is there anything I can do to prolong my vision?"

"There was a case study with Vitamin A Palmitate. 10,000 IU per day. That's good stuff. Some of the people retained their vision for five years longer. Some side effects, but minor…."

"Can you send me the link to that study? Or can you print it out?"

"Check back with my receptionist," he said vaguely, sounding somewhat irritated. I remembered that he didn't like paperwork, which made me smile. Like a drum majorette, I twirled the new information around in my head—this was the first time I'd heard it mentioned in degrees—and figured they only did that when it reached the low numbers. I guess that's why God made sure I was doing this mobility training with Bob.

Seated across from Doc Pritchard, I made the decision to adjust to my situation. Aside from rest, I'd focus on good nutrition and perhaps adding Vitamin A Palmitate to my daily diet, I couldn't do anything about my RP. I'd known for twenty-five years that I was losing my vision. So, it wasn't unexpected. After all, numbers didn't mean much. What really mattered was that I had the best non-yellowed nerve ending in the West.

"Do you have any questions?"

"No, I think my situation is clear."

He walked out of my line of vision for a second. It didn't take much for that to happen. I heard him say, "Come here. I want you to meet someone."

Doc Pritchard reappeared with a young woman who looked twenty or so. "This is my daughter. She speaks Spanish, too, and lived in Europe for awhile." He looked over at his daughter with pride. "Amy is a patient with RP. That is a progressive disease, so what it means for her is that she is losing her sight." His voice had taken on an explanatory tone.

"Daddy," she interjected, "I know what that is."

"Fair enough," he replied, and chose the short version, "Amy has like 20/200 vision—think of a horse with blinders—but a 20/20 attitude."

My ears pricked up at the compliment as he went on to explain the obstacles that I faced. I believe my head puffed up three times its size that day.

Around some people like Mrs. Curtis or Doc Pritchard—those I knew who supported and admired my effort to remain positive—it was easy to show that side of myself. It was harder when I was around people who spouted words like "blindness" and "cane." That was when I was put to the test.

Buoyed by Doc Pritchard's compliment, I shrugged into my coat and stuffed my now swollen head into my hat (it was feeling pretty tight with my ego vying for space with my brain). I floated on air out of his office and down his steps. I wonder if my feet ever touched the ground.

But they must have. I walked straight into a snow mound, which I somersaulted through, and landed in a wet crumpled heap at the foot of the road. With a little jump, I brushed off my clothes and swiveled toward the office entrance to see if anyone had seen my blunder. I could always blame my red face on the cold snow, couldn't I?

Me with my 20/200 vision…too little vision and too much vanity!

God chooses his own way to humble us with humor. His comic timing is impeccable.

But I knew that cantankerous Doc Pritchard with his bad comic timing and his big heart would get a kick out of watching me walk smack into a snow mound, tumble over, pick myself up and laugh it off.

"I'm not going to run from words that frighten me anymore. I'm going to face them courageously and be grateful for what I have," I whispered to myself and began my walk home.

I aimed to keep my 20/20 attitude even when my 20/200 vision changed. After all, numbers didn't mean anything. I had my doctor's word on that.

Chapter 13
All Things Spanish

"María, is it a one-time completed action or a repeated action?" I asked. "Look again."

"Oh, repeated."

"And does the verb have an AR, ER or IR ending?"

"AR," she said immediately.

"Is the subject singular or plural?"

She scrunched up her face. "Plural. So would it be *hablaban*?"

"Sí. You got it!"

A smile came over María's face. She coquettishly stuck out her tongue at Rudolfo, who teased her at every opportunity. It seemed he had a crush on her. She repeated the entire sentence correctly as she peeked over at him while I listened to her intonation—what I could hear of it, anyway.

Oh, to be that age again.

Granted, since I only taught them Spanish, I didn't know them as well as the other teachers did, but we had reached the point where their personalities were emerging.

I no longer dreaded teaching them grammar. As my Spanish fell into place,

I found no difficulty explaining the concepts or later reviewing them. We still spoke too much English in class, but I looked forward to teaching them.

In the evenings, I dangled my legs from the high stool at the breakfast bar and graded their homework. Could there be anything better than spending time with my dog and a handful of nacho chips dipped into the occasional bowl of chunky salsa? I often lost myself in the beautiful sounds of the Spanish words that resonated in my head as I corrected them on paper. Circling a wrong tense here or adding an accent mark there, I savored this quiet time working with language in the same room with Buddy, his breath warm on my feet. Finally losing hope that I'd drop a chip, he'd stretch out on the smooth tile and fall asleep. His regular breathing filled the air.

"Ah, Buddy," I said one evening as I scooted down next to him on the floor and stroked his silky black ears. *"La cucaracha, la cucaracha ya no puede caminar."* I searched my mind for the rest of the lyrics. *"Porque no tiene, porque le falta una pata de atras."* It had such an upbeat tune and was a favorite not only from my high school days, but with my students, who begged to sing it.

I gently nudged my dog's leg. "Buddy, guess what this song is about." He cocked his head and searched for the real meaning of life—nacho chips—as if he were more interested in his stomach than the song. "Ha! It's about a cockroach that can't walk because it doesn't have a hind leg."

Buddy's tail thumped against the stool. His eyes followed me as he picked up on my excitement. He jumped up as I danced, *estilo-Colombiano*, around the room singing the first stanza again. With one hand over my heart and the other out for balance, I shimmied my hips—or maybe it was my behind since I had no real hips to speak of and, come to think of it, no real sense of rhythm—belting out *"La cucaracha, la cuca-"*

As I tilted my face up, it crashed into the open cupboard door.

I bent over double and crumpled onto the tiled kitchen floor. Clutching my forehead, I sucked in my breath and let it out slowly.

Ohhhhh. My throbbing head.

I felt a nudge and a rough tongue against the top of my hand. Oh, Buddy. I felt another nudge, and put my arm around his neck, drawing him closer, needing his soft nuzzles. His dark eyes sought to console.

"Buddy," I whispered, "I was laughing at the cockroach with no hind leg when all the time I forgot that I can't even see."

The dog licked my hand again, as if to say, "That doesn't matter." I think he would have liked to see me dance more, but I couldn't muster the strength. He let out a deep, heartfelt doggy sigh as if he understood perfectly.

I wobbled as I tried to stand. Gaining strength, I darted into the bathroom and peered into the mirror. Two large bumps swelled with a slender red dotted slit between the two. I traced the first, larger lump and then the second with two fingers. Great! Nothing like camel humps on my forehead.

Back in the kitchen, I sat at the top of the steps and patted the floor. Buddy padded over and laid his head across my lap. "Serves me right, Buddy-Lou," I said, using my older brother's pet name for my favorite companion. "Next time I dance, remind me to close the cupboard door."

Fat chance. Out of sight, out of mind. Because I didn't usually see the cupboard door, I almost never remembered to close it. The same went for the door to the microwave. How many times had I smacked it with my head? Too many to count.

"La cucaracha, la cucaracha ya no puede caminar," I sang softly, burying my face in Buddy's dark fur.

Ppfft! His small, stray black hairs tickled me as they clung to my skin. I wiped my face several times to rid myself of them. Just my luck. "Silly dog. We need to brush you."

A few days later, I concentrated on Monday's lesson. I sat, again, at my breakfast-bar-turned-office, squinting at the page. Was there an accent over *solo*? The text looked a little out-of-focus but what bugged me was not knowing if this word had an accent mark or not. *"SO-lo. Solo."* I leaned into the book and rubbed the page with my fingernail, trying to make it clearer. But the word remained just as blurry.

That's when the true nature of the problem hit me. I ran down the stairs. "Mom! I can't see the accent marks anymore!" My heart raced. My legs felt rubbery. For a second, I feared I was moving so fast that I'd fall down the last couple of steps—but caught myself in time.

"Mom!"

"Stop hollering. I'm in the kitchen. If you want to talk to me, come here."

Chop. Chop. Chop. What was she doing?

"Mom, I can't find the accent marks anymore," I cried.

She paused, her knife a few inches over the cutting board. "What are you missing?"

"No, Mom. I can't *see* the accent marks in the Spanish book anymore." I raised my voice so she could hear me better.

She wrinkled her nose. "What's wrong with the Spanish book?"

"Mom, listen." I slowed down to enunciate. "The accent marks over the Spanish words. I can't see them anymore."

"Why not?"

Wasn't it obvious? "I'm losing *more* vision." Spanish II was not that big of a problem. But I started to tear up, thinking of all the literature I still had to teach to my one and only Spanish III student. All the verb tense endings in the plays we read would pose an enormous problem. I could never remember or memorize them all.

My mother put down her knife. She turned toward me, her face creased in soft caring lines. "I'm sorry, honey."

I pulled out a chair. "Just one more thing to worry about." My stomach knotted up. More changes.

My brother wandered into the kitchen. The air in the room was super-charged. He looked from me to my mother. "What's going on?"

"Amy's lost more vision."

"Huh?"

I explained about the accent marks. "Now what am I going to do?"

"I don't know about Spanish or accent marks, but don't you have that two-thousand-dollar machine the Blindness place gave you a few months ago? Isn't it supposed to make the print larger?"

I lifted my head. I had forgotten about that. "Yeah, but I don't really know how to use it. It's kind of complicated." As I spoke, the words from the sales-man, Dan something-or-other from Ohio, popped into my head. "*The beautiful thing about this piece of equipment is that it's so simple anyone can use it.*"

"I'd ask someone if I were you. It was free," he reminded. "And it's not doing any good just sitting there."

"Yeah, you're right. Thanks."

I'd have to call Dan what's-his-name if I wanted to learn how to operate it again. I wondered if I could find his contact details. Where had I put that paper?

Or I could just look up the word *solo* on the computer to see if it had an accent mark.

I brightened. Now that solutions were coming, I didn't feel quite so overwhelmed. "I guess I'm going to live."

"That's good to know," Mom said, picking up her knife and reaching for a carrot. "Supper's at five, so don't go wandering off. I'll need you to set the table."

❖ ❖ ❖

We had ten minutes of class remaining. I liked this part of the chapter where I modeled the pronunciation of a short paragraph called *Notas Culturales*. Cultural Notes. Normally, the students then broke up into pairs and practiced reading it aloud to each other. Afterward, we'd talk about the assigned topic. One of the boys, Rodolfo or sometimes Pedro, would say, "Do you have a story about that?"

As I read the cultural note that morning, the words disappeared from my vision. I halted, rubbing my eyes and staring at the book I held. The page looked blank. To cover my confusion, I said, "Can someone finish reading this?"

"Profesora, I will." Pablo picked up the reins and continued.

The disappearing-word act happened sometimes when I read silently, but this marked the first time it happened when I was modeling language in front of a class. A few minutes later, the words had magically reasserted themselves and the page looked normal.

Another lovely aspect of this disease.

I sighed. Reading seemed like a puzzle with a bit of wizardry included. When the disappearing act kicked in, a weird sensation came over my eyes and caused me to blink. It actually made me dizzy for a few seconds.

"Okay, what's this reading talking about?"

One student raised a hand. "It's about describing our appearance and especially about the face. It talked about the eyes. Different colors of eyes."

"Right," I assented. "And are eyes singular or plural in Spanish?"

Several students chorused, "Plural!"

"Funny," I mused, "Most eyes in Latin America are dark brown but in these text books they always bring up *ojos azules o ojos verdes*." Blue eyes or green eyes. "If a *latino* has eyes this color, they are very popular with their friends and family. When I lived in Colombia...."

"Here comes the story," someone whispered.

I smiled. "One of the American teachers had blue eyes and the other, green.

Everyone used to admire them. Strangers would even touch their blonde hair. When it came to me, a woman once said that I had *"ojos de caballo."*

The students gave me blank looks.

"Eyes of horse?"

"Yes, *horse eyes*. Think about it. It was a compliment of sorts." I laughed. "Horses have gentle eyes. I guess she was trying to find something good to say about my boring brown eyes."

The class giggled. Rudolfo turned to María. "You have *ojos de* squirrel— Profesora, how do you say squirrel in Spanish—Oh and, María, I mean that as a big compliment." He batted his eyes at her flirtatiously. "Squirrels have very gentle eyes."

María acted as if she would hit him on the spot. Sudden anger is akin to puppy love.

At dinner that evening, I shared what had happened to me in class. "I think what's going on is that the words on the page must have fallen under one of my missing pockets of vision and my good eye failed to see it. So, it just came out blank. Like air. Then when I shifted my eyes, my right eye compensated and the words came back. It's happening more frequently."

"Oh." My brother pointed to a container near me. "Can you pass the gravy?"

I picked up the gravy container and gave it to him. "Do you want some salad?" Mom asked. She held out the salad bowl to me.

Did anyone hear what I just said?

"No." I gripped the edge of the table. "I'm trying to explain to you guys what happened at work today."

Mom poured some raspberry vinaigrette on her greens. "I heard you. Well, maybe your sister will have some ideas about your vision. Have you talked to her about it?"

"I just told you what I think is going on." I glared.

"Well, don't get in a snit. I'm just saying she's pretty smart about things because she researches them on the Internet."

"I know. I know."

I made a mental note to ask my sister to research it if she had time and to also ask my ophthalmologist about this weird occurrence during the next appointment. He would be in the best position to explain what caused it.

Right now, I'll just think of it as my pretty horse eyes playing hide-n-seek. Or maybe I really mean trick-or-treat. I guess the trick comes first, and I get the treat when the words come back. At least that part's like magic, which is kind of cool. How many people can say they have magical, horse eyes?

God, I know you're with me. And you've given me this job so I'll trust that you'll keep my eyes in good enough working order to hold my position. Or you will help me learn to use that machine that Dan delivered to me from Ohio. Everything I experience gets filtered through you. So, whatever You allow is something I can cope with, right?

CHAPTER 14
CROSSING CITY STREETS

Completely blind, I stepped out into the city traffic. Just a few minutes earlier I had heard the sputtering of a diesel engine, or so I thought. I also caught the sound of squeaky bicycle parts followed by some young boys' chatter as they passed by. Since all my hearing antennae were fine-tuned, I noticed when several vehicles slowed down, and eventually came to a halt at the traffic light. I could tell by the thrum of engine noise without tire movement—all this coming from the street beside me. When these vehicles moved, I made sure that I moved, too.

I grasped my cane and rapidly made my way across the busy intersection, careful to sweep my cane in wide even arcs in the event I came across the raised bumps, which told me I had safely reached the opposite side of the road. On that occasion, I didn't sweep across any bumps for the blind. So I continued moving forward until my cane touched cement indicating the opposite curb. There, I held it straight up and down and tapped with the side of my cane until I found the top of the curb. Taking a big step, I found the grass, the sidewalk and finally, the section of raised bumps. That's when I stopped and waited.

My breath came quickly as if I'd been running, but really my body simply responded to the fight or flight syndrome of crossing the busiest intersection in the heart of downtown Erie while wearing my sleep shades. Laughter spilled out of me. I couldn't believe I had crossed State Street and not only that, but I led the way. "How'd I do, Bob?"

"Not bad, not bad at all. However, I would caution you to always pause a few seconds until you know for certain there aren't any vehicles in the turn lane. In the situation just now, there *was* a vehicle waiting to make a right-hand turn. Luckily, the driver was paying attention and waited patiently for you to cross before proceeding," Bob explained.

"Oh. Sorry!"

He continued the stern lecture. "Keep in mind, though, that not every driver will behave in such a kindly fashion. A lot of idiots will take these single-lane turns without even looking to see who could be in their path."

I hung my head. My actions could have hurt both Bob and me. "I remember you warned me earlier. All I could think about just now was that I didn't want to get caught in the cross traffic so I moved as fast as I could with the parallel traffic."

"Quite all right. I wouldn't have let you harm yourself. I knew the driver was waiting."

My mouth dropped open. "How did you know that, Bob?"

"A couple of ways. First, since I take my clients here often, I'm extremely familiar with these intersections. I know the traffic flow and patterns of all these streets. Second, I could hear the engine idling while the driver of that car waited beside the crossing. And mind you, I could also hear you take off and judge how far ahead of the car you walked. If I'd had any doubt for your safety, I'd have stopped you. Guaranteed."

I took a deep breath. "Okay, got it. I'll definitely remember to wait a few seconds, especially in downtown Erie."

Wow! There is so much to listen for and remember when crossing busy city streets. Thank you, God for not taking all my hearing away at once. I don't know how I'd ever cross the streets without it!

I couldn't begin to know the pressure Bob faced to ensure the safety of his "clients," as he called the people he trained. I knew that he was one of the few completely blind orientation and mobility instructors in the entire United States—and I had the privilege of being one of his clients.

God, You really chose the best for me, didn't you? Thank You for Your love and care! Not only is Bob super-qualified but he can also relate to my frustration of not seeing.

Now that Bob had made me aware of the danger, he relented. "But you moved confidently and found your way safely to the other side of the road, so I commend you. Ready to try again?"

"Yes, of course."

"Amy, our next task is to enter and leave one of the nearby financial institutions in the downtown district." He chuckled. I guessed that he had some banking business to complete, probably for the Bureau.

"Ready, Bob."

We didn't have to cross the road for this one, thank goodness.

"It's close. You're heading south now. You'll turn...."

"Just tell me right or left," I begged. I was getting confused with his cardinal directions.

"Okay, if you follow the walkway, you'll veer to the right. Feel the change with your cane. At the corner, turn left and walk until the sidewalk turns very smooth. You'll feel the difference with your cane. It's marble. When you feel that, slide your cane forward. You'll find the glass door. Reach out with your hand and find the handle. Then go in. I'm right behind you."

Concentrating, I did everything Bob said. I would have been fine had I not gotten tangled in the turnstile immediately inside the building. It took me a couple of minutes to extricate myself from the oddly-shaped bars and push my way through.

I had a feeling Bob had neglected to tell me about the turnstile on purpose. He wanted to test my problem-solving skills.

"I'll be right back," he said. "There's a bench near the wall. Why don't you have a seat?"

I found the wooden bench and sat down. Soon I discovered that I wasn't alone. To my right, I heard a crying baby and another noise I couldn't identify. Finally, I figured it out as the sound of a stroller wheeling back and forth while the mother hushed the baby. I listened for a few minutes, marveling at what I could discern without seeing.

"You're doing great," the woman said cheerfully. Was she talking to me or the baby who'd stopped crying? I waited, not sure if I should respond or not.

The woman continued. "Are you really blind?"

"Me? Well, kind of. Yeah. I mean, I'm *learning* how to be blind." That sounded ridiculous.

"Is that why you have that black mask over your eyes?"

"Yeah, it is." I didn't go around wearing masks for the fun of it.

"I admire you for getting through the turnstile. It's not something you expect, unless you're getting in line for a kiddie ride at Waldameer, is it?" I could hear her tinkling laughter. I fiddled with the strap of my sleep shades behind my head. What did this woman look like? I heard a cell phone ring and was left to my own devices to imagine the details of the woman and baby as she turned away to converse.

"Amy?"

I whipped around to the opposite direction when I heard Bob's voice. "Here I am."

"Splendid." He sounded full of energy. "We have one more task in today's mobility training session for you to complete. I presume you're ready?"

"Of course I am. What'll it be this time?"

"We're dropping off a bundle of Braille papers at the home of an associate. Your task is to locate the third floor apartment by whatever means you can."

I clapped my hands and exclaimed, "Bob, do you know Braille?"

"Certainly. Are you learning to type it?"

"Yes!"

As I stood up and unfolded my cane, I waved to the woman with the baby in the stroller just in case she was turned in my direction. She called out, "Stay determined! I'm rooting for ya' to be a great blind gal!"

I grinned. That sounded as ridiculous as my earlier comment. Funny, though, how a stranger's words could motivate and encourage me so much. *God, You always place people in my life to encourage me. I'm grateful for Your faithfulness.*

After I navigated myself back through the tricky boxed-in turnstile, I concentrated on Bob's instructions—again with the cardinal directions—and I constantly questioned if he meant right or left. Finally, we made it to the building and entered.

"Have you learned numbers in Braille yet?"

"Yep." I was glad to show off. "One through ten."

"Outstanding. Use your knowledge of Braille to locate the third floor."

Could I do it? I never thought about Braille outside of the practice sessions with Fran. Suddenly, I had a real-life use for it. Inside the elevator, I mentally began picturing the dots. Braille uses a series of six dots in two rows of three. I tried to recall the combination, which would indicate that a number would follow. It looked like a backwards L. Yes, that was it. I remembered because I thought it odd that numbers would be denoted at the start with a combination of dots that looked like an L, the start of the word "letter."

I racked my brain to remember the actual numbers. Didn't a single dot mean the number one? Two dots shaped like a colon meant the number two. Wasn't it two dots (the first and fourth dot in the series) that felt like two eyes that indicated the number three? I slowly found the wall with the buttons and felt for the Braille. I ran my fingers over it several times and punched a button.

As soon as I pressed the button, I doubted myself. I asked, "Bob, that was the third floor, wasn't it?"

"We'll soon find out."

I held my breath. My goodness! It wasn't a big deal. If I were wrong, we would just return to the elevator and try again.

God, I want to be right. Help me to have remembered correctly.

We got off the elevator. "If you pressed the right floor, the apartment is straight ahead," Bob said. He rang the doorbell.

From the exchange of conversation between Bob and the one who answered the door, I figured out that I'd located the right floor. My heart sang.

I did it! I did it! Hey, I did it! I read Braille in a real-life situation!

When we made it back down to the street, Bob told me his driver and the driver's wife would be waiting in the van just outside the entrance.

I heard a voice call, "Bob. Over here."

"The van is at the curb," my trainer said.

"All right." I practically skipped to the van. Good thing I didn't trip over my cane in the process.

I found the van easily enough and felt for the handle to the back seat. Right away, I threw it open. "You guys, I crossed State Street and even though I forgot about the turning lane, I lived to tell the tale. Guess what else? I made it through a really tough turnstile just inside the bank and this lady, practically a stranger, said I did a great job. And I even read Braille," I announced to them as if they were my best friends.

"Well, I'll be darned," said the driver's wife.

Suddenly, I remembered my sleep shades and removed them, just in time to see the driver's big smile as he patted Bob on the back. "I guess today's mobility lesson was a success."

"Bob, can I write something in Braille for you? Like a poem. Yes, I have a poem I want to share. Would you mind reading it? That'll give me a reason to practice. I've never written anything yet...."

Anything seemed possible that afternoon. For just a moment, my fears about losing my vision receded. All I could imagine was that I was mastering another new language, and I would be able to get around just fine. Hadn't I crossed the busiest street in the city without any vision at all?

"Whoa. Yes, I'm certainly willing to examine your Braille upon our subsequent orientation and mobility lesson—without a doubt. It seems poetry is among your list of fine accomplishments." He looked in my general direction with approval. "However, let's backtrack for just a moment and discuss today's mobility lesson before we arrive at your family residence. Would that suit you?"

"Of course!"

While we chatted, a verse popped into the back of my mind. Was it in Hebrews? I couldn't remember it word for word, but it seemed to me to be something about land and rain and crops.

I looked outside my window—a window I thanked the Lord I still had the ability to see through—and found the sun shining. I knew the rain had fallen on me, and I was going to produce a good crop. Crop. Yes, there was something in that scripture about crops.

When we arrived home, I thanked Bob, his driver, and the driver's wife. I hummed to myself as I entered my apartment, twirling in a circle when I reached my door. Over dinner, I told my family all about that day's mobility lesson.

My brother helped himself to some fries. "That's really good. I think Bob is pretty cool to teach you since he can't see and all."

I thought so, too.

Later that night I sought the scripture that kept niggling at the back of my mind. I turned to my Bible concordance and looked up *crop*. I glanced through the snippet of information, and then turned to the passage.

*Land that drinks in the rain often falling on it and that
produces a crop useful to those for whom it is farmed
receives the blessing of God.*

Hebrews 6:7

*God, I think You're speaking to me right now, but how does this apply to
my situation? Are You saying that if I look at everything I'm going through as
something that will nourish me, my life will bring forth a crop—the fruit of the
spirit—to bless me? My family? Others? You?*

*Oh, Lord, it's so, so difficult to imagine my life without seeing even tiny
seemingly insignificant details like the accent marks in my Spanish book. It's
really happening to me. It's not in a bad dream. It's in real life. It seems like
every day I'm losing another fragment of my vision. I'm scared, God, to lose
my independence.*

*But despite my fear, I want to grow a good crop for You, be blessed, and
bless others. God, show me how. Thank You for Bob and his willingness to teach
me how to be "a great blind gal."*

*Tomorrow, I'm going to take my stylus and my slate. I'm going to write my
poem not in Spanish, or Japanese, or Arabic. I'm going to write it in Braille, in
the language You're providing me with right now. I know it's not Bob's job to
help me with my Braille, but thank You that he's willing to take on that task in
addition to my mobility training.*

With that decision made, I fluffed up my pillow and tried to still my heart
so that I could get a good night's sleep.

Chapter 15
STARTING SMALL

The next morning, I jumped out of bed and finished my chores in record time. I had prepared for my classes in advance and still had some time before leaving for work, so I fumbled through my desk drawer until I came up with my slate and stylus. "Buddy, where's the first book?" I asked, bending over to ruffle his fur. "Oh, there it is in my bookshelf."

I lugged the spiral-bound book to my kitchen "office," scooted up on the stool and opened to the alphabet. The outline of the oversized letters in black marker showed clearly as my fingers reviewed the dots. I deciphered which letter went along with each set of dots.

Who would ever have believed that one day I'd be learning a second language consisting of only embossed dots? When I had unusual experiences growing up, Dad used to say, "Put that on your resume." I wished he could see me now. He would be proud.

When I flipped to the practice pages, my fingers hesitated, and I felt each set of dots slowly. In between letters, two small embossed lines declared that a new letter was coming. It took a lot of concentration.

"That's enough for one day, Buddy. I have to get to work."

As I made copies of handouts for my lesson, Mrs. Curtis walked into the school office. "Good morning, Amy," she said brightly.

"Good morning."

She walked to the filing cabinet, pulled out a couple of files and headed back to her office.

I gathered up my copies and left. On the way back, I peeked into her office. "Do you have a sec?"

"Sure, what is it?"

I felt like I was glowing. "I just wanted to tell you about my mobility training. I completed another session yesterday, and you wouldn't believe how it went." My words tumbled out. Halfway through, I drew up a chair and sat down on the other side of her desk.

I continued to talk until finally I told her all the adventures I experienced with my cane the day before. Throughout, she nodded and asked a question here and there. She gave me her full attention. I loved that about her.

"I'm so sorry to take up your time. I just wanted to share that with you."

"Not at all," she said. "It's a thrill to hear you so enthusiastic."

"I know." I clasped my hands together. "Your prayers are working, Mrs. Curtis." I stood up and placed the chair in its spot near the door. "I don't know if I could do *any* of this if Bob were not watching out for me. So I definitely haven't made the step to be self-sufficient yet. But I can't believe how much progress I'm making."

She hesitated. "Have you thought any more about speaking to the high school students in Chapel?"

I didn't say anything at first. "No, I'm just … well, it's … some of the students don't even know me."

She looked intently at me. "Have you told any of your students yet?"

"Um, no. There's no time to go into it all. We have an exam coming up shortly."

She nodded, looked down at her papers, and began to shuffle them.

Was that disappointment in her eyes? Was she dismissing me? Did she think I was a coward?

I stood, unsure if I should leave her office on this note. Should I apologize because I talked a good talk but couldn't—or wouldn't—take it to the next level?

"Mrs. Curtis? I'll uh…think about it. Maybe I could try…just not so sure…." My voice trailed away. I knew time was running out. But what a big commitment! I wasn't *ready*.

All the students would stare. What would they think as I told them about my biggest failure? Shivers ran up my arm and my stomach felt queasy. The bell rang, and I backed out of the office, nearly knocking over a student in my haste.

I heard the principal say in a cheery voice, "How can I help you today, Sharon?"

Just before I left school that day, Mrs. Curtis stuck her head through my classroom door. "Just some words for thought," she said. "Start small." With an encouraging smile, she left.

What did *that* mean?

Start small? Start *small*.

The strange phrase remained with me the whole afternoon. When Julio called, I told him about the exchange between Mrs. Curtis and me. I held the phone to my ear as I dried and put away the dishes.

"Obviously, she wants you to do the talk."

The silverware clattered as I dropped a fork and spoon. "But Julio, I don't know if I can."

He groaned. "What are you doing? That hurt my ear." He didn't wait for me to answer before he rushed into his next spiel. "And you're asking the wrong person. I'm three thousand miles away in California. How am I supposed to know? Ask *her* what she means."

I persisted. "Does she mean that the high school students are a small group?"

"Well, your entire student body is less than a hundred, isn't it? So the high school section must be really small."

"Yeah, but…."

"You're a teacher. Just tell them what you're facing. How hard can that be?"

I wiped some water off the rim of a glass with a dish towel and set it in the cupboard. "Well, teachers are not speakers."

"Oh, right. I forgot. Teachers lead the class silently. The next thing you're going to say is they do it through sign language." I heard Julio call out a greeting to someone on campus. "Hey, I need to go now," he said. "Call you later."

That night when I went to sleep, I prayed for guidance.

Lord, tell me what to do. Although I am making progress, why do I have to put myself even more on display? And please help me understand what Mrs. Curtis meant.

I woke up, sweating. I threw off my covers and checked the time. The luminescent numbers indicated it was four a.m. A thought came to mind. *Speak to Piedad.*

Was my one and only student in my Spanish literature class God's answer to my prayer?

I flopped back down in bed, covering myself only with a light blanket and thought about how I would share my story with her and still use Spanish. Every Friday we stepped away from our syllabus and read devotionals from Max Lucado's *Un Cafecito Con Max.* (the Spanish version of *Mocha With Max*).

We looked at the native-level sentence structures and vocabulary and figured out the meaning together.

What about if I treated my situation with RP in the same way? I could teach Piedad the vocabulary dealing with vision and whatever other words I needed to explain my condition. *Like blind.* I winced. In Spanish, it sounded even worse: *ciega.* In Spanish literature, it often referred to a destitute, old, and an either ill-mannered or helpless blind woman.

You're not any of those things, except blind, so stop psyching yourself out.

Start small. One student. One class period.

Sure, I could do that. I had a day to prepare myself. Friday wasn't until the day after tomorrow.

I came to class armed that Friday with several teaching tools: two Braille alphabet cards, my cane, a special adjustable lens called a monocle—perhaps Piedad might like to try it out—and a list of new terms.

My heart beat faster as Piedad entered the classroom and took her seat. She looked curious when she saw the various objects on the desk across from her but she waited politely for me to speak.

Okay, profesora, here we go.

Piedad listened carefully, asked questions and looked up the unfamiliar words or listened to my simple explanations in Spanish.

"I love those little cards in Braille!" she exclaimed, picking one up and examining it closely. "Can you really read this?"

In Spanish, I told her I was learning it now.

"Cool!"

I smiled at her responses and handed her my monocle. She held it up to her eye and turned the black casing back and forth.

I gave her permission to take a walk with it. She took a few steps and hurriedly sat back down and placed the monocle on the desk. "That's weird. It makes my eye tired and a little dizzy. What do you use it for?"

I lapsed into English for a moment. "It's for finding house addresses and the prices of merchandise in stores. But I haven't used it yet."

We returned to our Spanish instruction for the remainder of the class session.

"*Adiós*, Profesora," she said shyly, tossing her long straight hair over her shoulder. "*¡Gracías!*"

Relieved to have finished the class, I realized that I could never go back to the way I used to be. Piedad would probably tell others and more and more students would learn about my vision loss. But would they know the truth? And how would their parents react?

Buck up, *chica*, you just might have to give that talk in Chapel before school lets out. Would that be so bad? I had no answer. May was upon us. I knew I'd have to make up my mind soon.

The following week, Mrs. Curtis came to my classroom. She looked apologetic. "Amy, I'm sorry not to give you any notice, but I'm required to observe all first-year hires. Would you mind if I sit in on your class for a little bit?"

"Of course not. Can someone please find Mrs. Curtis a chair?"

She waved away the help and quietly took an empty seat in one of the back rows.

Outwardly, I cultivated a façade of calm. Inside, I panicked. I'd always scored high ratings in my teacher observations. But now everything was different. What if I stumbled over one of the student's books? Or what if a student asked if there was an accent mark on a particular word?

The purpose is to observe a typical class, so that's what I'll give her.

Afterward, the principal stayed for a few minutes to talk.

"Good class," she said immediately. "I just have a slight concern that you may not have heard the responses of all your students. Were you aware of that? For example, I don't know what you call her in Spanish but she was the last girl in the third row. She has a very quiet voice. I don't think you heard her."

"María? Carolina? No, I think that must have been Nora. No, I wasn't aware I missed her response today. Sorry." I so wanted her to think highly of my teaching.

"I noticed it happened a couple of times," she said gently. "What do you usually do when you don't hear a student's response?"

"I usually ask the quieter students to repeat themselves."

She held her pen at an angle and tapped it against her lips, in typical problem-solving mode. "And if he or she still doesn't speak any louder?"

"Well, I try to walk around so I hear them better. I just didn't do that today. Um, because I didn't want to trip over any books," I admitted.

"Okay." She paused for a moment. "What about if we move your teacher's desk to the back left-hand corner of the room to allow you some more space to walk in front? Do you think that would help?"

I looked in the direction she indicated. "That might work out."

"You also need to make it clear to the students that you expect their books to be under their chairs at all times."

"Yes, I really, yeah, I do need to enforce that."

I bit my lip, ashamed of my poor hearing. The negative voices we all carry around in our heads attacked. *You should have stopped teaching years ago! How did you ever think you'd be a successful language teacher? You're deaf, you know. And the way you manage your class is pitiful.*

"Let's see if we can move the desk ourselves," Mrs. Curtis suggested, pushing up her sleeves.

I stood on one end and lifted while she picked up the other. A few minutes later, the classroom was rearranged.

"There," she said, straightening the angle of the desk. "Let me know if you need anything else from me. I'll be happy to strategize with you."

"Thank you so much," I said humbly.

"You're welcome." She took a step toward the door. "We're in this together, Amy. God wants to use all of us to the best of our abilities. Even when things don't go as planned, God has His reasons. So don't let it get you down. Just go forward."

I could feel a lump forming in my throat. Tears welled up in the corners of my eyes and I tried to smile at her. She seemed to know exactly how I felt.

The door shut behind her. I sat down at my desk looking around my classroom from my new vantage point. I took in my Spanish travel posters, the colorful bulletin board I changed every time we started a new chapter. Next to the bookshelf sat the smooth, brown and tan coil-woven basket I'd bought at the *mercado* in Colombia. On its lid, I'd placed a hand-sewn Mexican doll. A Costa Rican *flauta* (flute) in the shape of a bird decorated one of the shelves along with an Ecuadorian boat carved from stone.

We have a good learning environment, I told myself. Mrs. Curtis knew that I cared about my classes. We were a team, a Godly team.

As I gathered up my books to leave, I recalled how whenever the teachers had a brunch, our principal circled the table. She would offer a beverage choice to each person, and poured it herself.

Today, she took the same personal approach and poured encouragement into my empty glass.

Chapter 16
Observing...¡Silencio!

One morning, I woke up with a sore throat and blocked ears. But I had only two classes to teach, so I decided to go into work.

In my Spanish II class, Carolina came up to my desk and whispered something that seemed important by the way she bent in and gestured toward the whiteboard. I couldn't quite make out what she said, though, since she was speaking through her braces.

I tapped my hearing aid and three little bells sounded indicating it was set at the highest level. "Excuse me, Carolina. Can you say that again?"

No better the second time around. I was forced to say, "Sorry, I didn't catch what you said."

Carolina rolled her eyes and sucked air through her metal braces. But she leaned in and whispered again. Whispering was difficult to follow on the best of days but that day I felt especially awful and everything sounded muffled.

Did the students even know I wore hearing aids? They were tiny, sophisticated devices that I could hide behind my ears. Nothing showed except for the slender clear wire that held them on. I'd never mentioned wearing them to the students. At their best, however, they brought my hearing to ninety-one percent.

So, even on good days, I couldn't fully hear quiet sounds.

When I couldn't hear Carolina the third time, pride got the better of me, and I nodded as if I had, giving her a reassuring smile.

Typical of me.

My mother, hard of hearing because of her age, never let anything pass. She insisted on repetition until she understood whatever was said. I wish I had that discipline or really, her tenacity. I gave up far too easily and let a lot of what I missed slide. I think I learned that from my dad, who was deaf in one ear due to running the chain saw most of his life. I remember all the times we talked to him and he just smiled and grunted. If Mom hadn't reminded us we were speaking to his bad ear, we would have never known.

I looked at the whiteboard hoping it would give me clues as to what Carolina had meant by her whisper. She smiled at me and returned to her seat with a happy gait, having accomplished her mission.

Our lesson took up most of the class and I completely forgot about whatever Carolina had tried to tell me. But at a couple minutes to eleven, she began to cough and point frantically to the clock on the wall. I looked at the clock. We still had about ten minutes of class left, so I continued with our lesson. The class took a lively interest in the dramatic show of attention the time received. I re-directed their attention to the class activity at hand.

"*¡Por favor, silencio!*" I admonished.

"*Sí, sí!*" they shouted, "*¡Silencio!*"

A wave of "*Silencios*" tore through the classroom, accompanied by several sets of double arms waving up and down and pointing to the clock in fairly synchronized movements. But with my vision, the arms looked fuzzy to me. What was everyone trying to say? Did I miss a fire drill?

It seemed like a comedic pantomime.

I stared at my students. *Han ido todos locos?* Had they all gone mad?

"What's going on?" I said, perplexed. "Come on. Let's finish our lesson.

We're almost done." I turned back to our textbook, which I placed on a music stand that served as my podium. In retrospect, this was much too fragile a piece of equipment to ever hold a book in place.

As I tried to stop the drama, I grew flustered and pushed the page of the teacher's text a bit too hard to emphasize my desire to get back to work. The music stand slid two inches lower. When I tried to pull it up again, my wrist caught the leg of the stand, and I threw it backwards. With a thud, it bounced off the whiteboard, and crashed sideways to the floor. The teacher's text slid three feet to the right, upside down.

But it didn't stop there.

I tripped over the base of the music stand and pitched sideways into a special desk that held a fan—which happened to be turned on. The black marker I was holding flew toward the fan. For one terrible moment, I feared that the marker would get sucked into the blades.

The worst case scenario came to mind. The sound of the blade chewing up the marker would echo out my open window to the old "empty" sanctuary on the other side. That racket would then reverberate to the principal's office. In turn, she would run to my classroom, throw open the door and shout, "Oh my goodness. What a racket!"

Much to my relief, the fan didn't chew up the marker. It ricocheted off the blades. Even so, I needed to sit down. I felt my way to a chair, and someone, I think Pedro, stepped over to me. "Are you okay, *Profesora*?"

I rolled my eyes and gave him a thumb's up sign. I'd had better moments, for sure, but considering the marker was intact and the principal hadn't come, things could have been worse.

My hearing aid suddenly picked up all kinds of sounds and magnified them, mostly the peals of laughter coming from my students' open mouths.

"Bet you didn't know your *profesora* could do comedy, did you?" *We all need a little levity now and again.* I checked for bruising or broken bones.

María picked up my teacher's book and handed it to me. Rudolfo quickly followed suit and set the music stand upright. They gave each other a high-five for their teamwork.

The class finally settled down enough for me to speak.

"Why were you waving your arms and acting so crazy? Obviously you were trying to tell me something. Why didn't someone just come out and say it?"

Carolina said, "I *told* you. I mean, I asked for permission. You said we could. Remember at the start of class? We had to observe a moment of silence at exactly eleven o'clock because everyone in the United States is supposed to do that at the same time. The president said so. Now it's too late!" She pouted.

"Oh, I get it. So that's what you said. *Vamos a hacerlo ahora.* Let's observe the silence now."

Of course, as soon as the words left my mouth, the bell rang.

That set off my students all over again. In small groups and still laughing, they gathered their books together and left the room. They lucked out. No homework.

The music stand stood off by itself without the book in its usual place. It made me smile. While I still hadn't shared my hearing problems directly with the students, our collective response had changed. It made us laugh where once the students had been bewildered, and I had wanted to cry. Mrs. Curtis's talk bolstered my confidence. I would just go with the flow today.

I thought of that old saying, "Silence is golden." Not in my classroom. Our *silencio* was the noisiest we'd ever heard.

Except for me.

Chapter 17
A deeper commitment

"You're really making progress with your Braille," exclaimed Fran. "It's a shame our training stops here."

"It does? Bummer."

"You suddenly took off. It happens that way sometimes. I just wish...."

I looked away. I knew exactly when I took off. It was when Bob bumped me into gear. Before that, I would cram for half an hour before Fran arrived. So, when I read the Braille aloud to her, I often stumbled over the letters. It seemed strange that "sounding out" the letters meant running my fingers over them several times.

Fran closed the book slowly. "It might not have to stop. Are you interested in learning Braille in a more intensive program? We can provide additional training for you if we can prove that it will help you succeed in job employment opportunities."

"Well, I'm a teacher. Maybe if I learn Braille, I can turn around and teach it."

She thought that over. "It's a possibility. My job is to introduce Braille as a resource, and I've done that. What you do with your new skills is up to you.

But in order to press for the training, we will have to link it to job retention or new hiring possibilities." She paused. "Are you really interested?"

"Yes. Is the training in Erie?"

"No. However, there are several cities around that do offer intensive training. There's a center in Pittsburgh and another in Cleveland. But usually a candidate attends the course for a year, or at the very minimum, six to eight months. The training doesn't just involve Braille. It consists of life skills classes, orientation and mobility training, and specialized computer training, usually with JAWS. Have you heard of that program?"

"Yes. David used that screen reader to help him assemble my computer." My face fell. "Six or eight months! I can't take off work that long. I'd lose my job."

"And if the whole purpose is to keep you employed, that's counter-productive."

"Well, thanks anyway for your time and sharing your expertise with me," I said glumly. "I'll try to keep going on my own." I hoped I could keep myself motivated.

I had applied myself to becoming more adept at reading Braille but put off attempting to write. "Today's the day," I said to Buddy as I found my slate and stylus. "I need to have this finished when Bob comes."

Mom peeked into my apartment. "What are you doing?"

"Attempting to write in Braille." I picked up my tools and showed them to her. "This pointy instrument is what I make the dots with," I said, holding up the stylus.

"It looks like part of a nail," she observed.

"Yeah, kind of, except the point is not as sharp." I held up a sheet of thick crème-colored paper and slid it into the narrow rectangular tin contraption with holes across it. "I put my paper in here. This is called the *slate*."

Mom leaned in to see the operation better.

"Then I punch the dots in the right position. Mom, the whole alphabet is based on different combinations of only six dots. Can you imagine?"

"Sounds complicated." She made a face and backed away.

"It's really not," I said as if I were an expert and not a novice who had yet to attempt a single dot. "I want to show Bob what I can do," I said.

Mom shook her head, slightly confused. "Does he teach you Braille, too? I thought he just taught you how to walk."

I rolled my eyes. "Mom! I know how to walk. He's teaching me the ins and outs of using a cane. Big difference."

She sniffed and cocked her head to one side. "Hoity-toity, there."

"Sorry, Mom." I grinned at our war of words. "Bob said that he'd look at it. I want to copy a poem," I said, excited at being creative. Typical. I wanted to be fancy without knowing if I could even do the basics. "He's coming tomorrow."

"Seems to me you're almost as excited about showing him your Braille as you are about your training session," she said, laughing.

"Ha ha! More. You know how much I love languages."

"Is Braille a language?"

"Of course it is. Well, a written language," I amended.

I could hardly wait for Bob to arrive. We would practice crossing more city streets, and I would learn about possible bus routes and taking buses, which seemed rather impractical since the bus service to my area was limited to once a week. My hometown was considered rural. But, of course, any training would benefit me.

When Bob and his driver arrived, I was waiting in the driveway. "Got my sleep shades right here along with my Braille," I called out, waving the thick cream-colored sheets in the air.

"Braille?"

"Yeah, remember, you promised to read through some of my practice," I reminded.

"Yes, indeed. I had forgotten."

I slid the van door shut and folded up my cane. I still didn't use it very much, but I definitely used it in front of Bob. "Hey there, Roger," I said to the driver.

After Bob explained more about the lesson, I handed him the papers to read.

Bob leaned back in the car seat. "Hmm. Yes, going through the alphabet, I see. An error here, you've reversed the H and the J. The dots face opposite directions from each other." The car hit a bump and jostled the paper. "I'm not certain this is the most appropriate time to be reading your work," he remarked.

"You, a master of Braille skills, can finish in a jiffy."

"Assumedly so," he smiled to deflect the flattery of my words. "After a lifetime of Braille practice. Here we go. The days of the week," he paused. "Uh-oh, another mistake. You wrote an I instead of an E on Tuesday. Easy enough to remedy, mind you. Yes, yes. Now you're practicing the months of the year."

"The second paper has my poem," I urged. "Halfway down, you'll find it."

Bob was not the kind of person to rush through anything, so I waited anxiously for him to read through my drills until he reached my poem. I found myself holding my breath as his fingers moved over the paper. How would he react to my poem? I wondered if he was still angry at God, blaming Him for her death.

When he flipped to the second sheet, he frowned. "What's this?"

"Huh?"

After a moment of silence, he said, "I can't read this. It doesn't say anything."

"What do you mean?" I wanted to grab the paper out of his hands. When I was looking through my poetry, I came across one that I wrote years earlier. As I read it over, it took on a different, deeper meaning in relation to my vision loss. God spoke to me through that poem, and I felt it was the one God wanted me to share. I had painstakingly copied it over, discarding it twice before I was satisfied there were no errors.

"I know what you did," he said slowly, "You've written the Braille from the wrong direction."

"What do you mean by that? Are you sure you can't read it?"

"It's impossible." He handed the papers back to me. "You'll have to write it over if you want me to read it," he added.

"Do it over?" I groaned. "That took me hours to do."

Bob interrupted our conversation to address his driver. "Roger, are we nearing the site?"

"Yes, sir. A couple of minutes more."

"Very good. We'll have plenty of time to complete the tasks I designed."

I felt the hard edge of paper on my fingertips and realized Bob was returning my Braille practice to me. "Amy, don't lose perspective. Whenever you invest time in developing a much-needed skill or even an interest, you will always reap the benefits."

I let out a long, exasperated sigh. Probably it wasn't the right time to share my poem. I would have to trust God to show me when that should happen.

Bob certainly had no idea I wanted to use the poem to witness to him. But the fact that he picked up on my sigh made me smile. He had such good listening skills. Bob must have taken my sigh as discouragement about Braille.

"Seriously. You committed a common error. Remember when you use a slate and stylus, you always start on the *right* side of the paper and work your way to the left. Then, when you turn the paper over to read it, the dots face the correct direction, from left to right."

"Oh, yes. I forgot. You turn it over to read it."

"This peculiarity is limited to the slate and stylus only. The Perkin's Brailler, on the other hand, can be typed from left to right, exactly as it's read."

"That's the typewriter for the blind, right?"

A couple words from Roger and the van came to a stop.

"It certainly is." Bob shifted his focus. "We have arrived at the desired crossroads for our mobility practice now. You *are* wearing your sleep shades, I presume."

"But, of course."

I slid the van door open and jumped onto the sidewalk, waiting for Bob to follow suit and deliver my first set of instructions. We encountered crowds as we made our way to the specific destination only Bob knew. Having so many people around helped because when the light changed, I could hear them and feel them surge forward. I established a kind of rhythm as I moved with them.

"Hang on, Bob," I panted, fanning myself. The sun—or maybe a hot flash—left me sweating. "I absolutely must take off this heavy sweatshirt."

I tied the sleeves around my waist and adjusted my sleep shades. The elastic sometimes felt loose. "Now, I'm ready."

"As I was saying, we shall enter a commercial building shortly. It will be your task to discover and report back regarding the type of business establishment and, if possible, the product it handles."

I loved the way Bob worded things so formally. He had a unique perspective and steely nerves. I had to think carefully if I wanted to complete the tasks he set for me. He didn't make it easy. On the contrary, he forced me to problem-solve and stretch my abilities.

After several directives, I found myself inside the building. I listened quietly to Bob's conversation with the owner or clerk, not sure which hat she wore. Then I walked around the large room, listening to other patrons. Some parts of the floor felt like hardwood. Others seemed so quiet I came to the conclusion that the area must be carpeted. I heard a cash register ping open and shut.

Bob spoke to the woman again, and she explained, "It hasn't come in yet, but I've ordered it. Are you sure it's available in Braille?"

Aha! Something written.

I sniffed. A smell hung in the air. Chicory? No. Richer. Something pleasant. "Coffee!" I said excitedly. What kind of store had both coffee and something written that hadn't come in yet.

A bookstore!

"Hey Bob, I've figured it out. It can't be a library because coffee is sold here. But it must have books, too. It's a bookstore."

"Excellent."

"This is one of my more industrious students," he said to the woman. "Amy, let me introduce you to the owner of the oldest bookstore in Erie. The Erie Bookstore is my absolute favorite hangout. I'm here as often as my schedule allows."

I could almost see Bob beaming.

The owner laughed. "It's because of loyal patrons like you that we have been able to remain open nearly one hundred years, young man." It sounded like she tapped the countertop. "You graciously find the time, so we have the honor of your presence along with that of your sweet wife almost daily."

They seemed to have a long history of friendship. For a second, I got a lump in my throat thinking that Bob chose to take me to a bookstore—and not only a bookstore, but his *favorite* one, and the oldest in the area—for part of our mobility lesson. It seemed auspicious, especially since one day I hoped to be a writer. Would my book grace these bookshelves one day?

"Amy, would you like a cup of coffee?"

I paused, torn in my decision. "No, that's all right." I said, finally. I wondered if I sounded disappointed or regretful. My face burned and when I touched my cheeks, they felt hot with embarrassment.

I couldn't find the words to casually ask who would pay for the coffee. I hadn't brought any money with me. How could I assume that Bob would pay? And we didn't have a casual enough relationship for me to ask.

I always regretted not taking that cup of coffee and relishing the ambiance of Erie's oldest bookstore with Bob. I should have celebrated my success in correctly identifying the kind of business it was. Moments like those never repeat themselves. I made a vow later to embrace such times and worry less about propriety.

God wants us to enjoy life. One of my favorite Bible verses reminds me of this, *"This is the day that the Lord has made. Rejoice and be glad in it. Again, I say rejoice."*

It is also written, *"You will eat the fruit of your labor; blessings and prosperity will be yours."* Sharing success over coffee would have qualified as eating (or, in our case, drinking) the fruit of our labor. Of course, if the bookstore sold bagels or muffins, we could have taken that verse literally and eaten them.

After we left, Bob gave me another set of instructions, and we made our way to a hectic bus stop. He showed me how to find out which bus I needed to take to reach various places and what I should ask the driver.

While we waited for the bus, I told him how Fran's Braille classes had finished. "She says that I can take more intense training. Bob, what do you think about that?"

"It's a capital idea. But, I would suggest taking several classes, not just Braille. In fact," his voice took on an eager edge, "you should consider being trained at the Louisiana School for the Blind. The curriculum and excellent faculty maximize your opportunities, though it takes a rather long time to finish."

"That's the problem. I have only the summer months free. I start teaching again in the fall."

"Did I tell you I received my Master's Degree at the Louisiana School for the Blind—or the LSB as we fondly called it—in Orientation and Mobility?" Bob went on to explain the requirements and, I suppose, relive his glory days. Why not? He had accomplished so much.

"Amy, if you go blind before I prepare you, I will never forgive myself," he said suddenly. "I cannot let that happen."

"No, don't worry. It's a slow progressive disease," I assured him.

"My hands are tied. I can only work with any one client once a month," he muttered. "The restrictions I face are in the broadest terms, maddening and in the narrowest, frustrating. The progress is slow, and I lose ground re-teaching what a client has forgotten over the month's time."

"Yeah, I can see why that would be difficult."

Bob had never opened up to me like this before.

God, please give him encouragement in the face of his frustrations. He has such a difficult job, and he wants to make a difference in his clients' lives.

Once Bob got it into his mind that I should attend LSB, he raved about the benefits I would receive. "I can personally recommend your case to the head of the school. You would make an excellent Orientation and Mobility instructor with the right training. This will provide stable future employment for you," he added.

"Me? Taking on a job like you have!" The thought had never entered my mind, and I did not share the certainty Bob had in me. Didn't I almost get us killed last time?

He warmed up to the topic. "LSB requires their students to take classes in rock climbing and wood crafting, the latter in which they operate drills and saws. In your case, you would wear sleep shades for all your classes and...."

It sounded exciting, though I wasn't sure I wanted to operate a saw, especially if it were an electric one, wearing sleep shades. My father, who ran a tree removal business, refused to allow me to operate a chain saw all the summers I worked for him. "Your mother would shoot me if I did and anything happened to you," he always said, sternly. That was one of the few things he never joked about on the job.

The bus training went smoothly. I even exited without a hitch.

On the way home, something clicked inside me, and I made up my mind to speak to the high school students. I explained this to Bob and invited him to join me. The occasion would provide the opportunity for me to honor him. "I'm not quite sure of the date, but will you come once I get that settled?" I pleaded.

"That's most kind of you to invite me," he said politely. "I'll have to let you know. It depends on the date selected and my schedule, which, to be frank, is usually overloaded."

"It'll be in the next couple of weeks. Our school finishes soon. I *really* hope you can come. I want everyone to meet you."

As soon as I spoke, I covered my mouth. Did I say that?

Yes, and I meant every word.

Chapter 18
LESSONS IN THE CHAPEL

"Mrs. Curtis, I've decided to speak to the high school students in Chapel if that's still something you want me to do," I said the next morning.

She didn't seem surprised by my announcement. "That can certainly be arranged. It will likely be toward the end of next week. We can rearrange our schedule so that Chapel is just before lunch." She sorted through her files until she found the proper paper. "Yes, it'll be on a Thursday, but we'll follow Wednesday's morning schedule."

"Terrific!" I said. "Would it be possible to invite Bob as well? I want him to hear how thankful I am to have him as my trainer."

I'd also like him to hear that God has used him to soften my fears about my future. But most of all, I want Bob to hear my testimony of God's faithfulness, not only in the face of this loss but how he has always provided for me, especially when I yielded to His will for me.

"He's certainly welcome to join us," she said without hesitation. "I'm so pleased you decided to share your testimony of God's faithfulness in your life. Students need to know they're going to come up against very real challenges that don't have any clear answers. We need to model faith in action and how to yield to His will in whatever circumstances He allows."

I stared at her. Her words echoed my thoughts almost word-for-word. This had to be a confirmation from God.

Before I prepared my talk, I prayed for God to show me what to focus on and share. Halfway through my planning, I called Rita, my counselor at the Bureau of Blindness, to explain that I would be giving a talk and to ask for some Braille resources.

"We can send you some cards with the alphabet on them," she offered. "That's about all we have on hand. You have a couple of books, right?"

"Uh-huh, and my slate and stylus. Magnifying glasses. My cane. Various cane tips. I don't think it would be wise to take in the CCTV, that big computer screen that enlarges print, though."

"Not a good idea," Rita agreed. "That's an expensive and very delicate piece of equipment. On second thought, it does have a carrying case. It's up to you."

"I think I'll leave it at home. I have that strange, bed-jarring alarm I can set up."

"What is that?"

"It's a sensor-operated digital alarm clock Fran recommended I order. Because it's for the hearing-impaired, when the alarm goes off, it shakes your bed. Believe me, it feels exactly like you're in an earthquake! The students will love it." I grinned, hoping I could remember how to activate the alarm. After only a few bed-shaking mornings, I had turned off that feature.

"That sounds like something the kids will enjoy." She chuckled. "Is there anything else I can help you with?"

"No, that about covers it, Rita."

The biggest disappointment was that Bob couldn't make it. He said he couldn't clear his calendar, especially since the school was located so far from his office and my chapel presentation took place in the morning.

God, I'm still waiting on your timing.

On the morning of my presentation, I suddenly became anxious. This was it. No more hiding. My vision and hearing problems would soon be out in the open. Even the students who didn't know me from my classes would now know *about* me. I wiped away the beads of sweat that formed on my neck. I was focusing on the wrong aspect. I was supposed to be challenging students to grow their faith. I reminded myself of how much support I had for this talk. Several members of my family would attend the presentation. My prayer warriors at church were praying for me. My friends had wished me luck, and even the team at the Bureau of Blindness rooted for me.

I arrived early to the chapel and set up my display. At that moment, the empty pews looked threatening. It's just nerves, I told myself sternly. I climbed the three shallow steps leading up to the podium and wobbled unsteadily as I sought the top step. Oh Lord, what if I fell in front of the students and faculty? Should I use my cane? No. It didn't require all that fuss to move from the first pew and then climb a few steps to the podium.

I took a deep breath to calm myself. God had placed these people in my life for me to bear witness to His faithful love and support. I could *do* this.

I found my twenty-five-year-old niece halfway up the center pew. She mouthed something to me, which I couldn't make out. I felt my clothing to be sure she wasn't saying I had on something backwards or inside out. Then she smiled, and I relaxed a little bit.

When I saw the high school students file into the chapel and take their seats,

I returned to the first pew, my heart thudding against my chest.

Mrs. Curtis gave me a warm welcome and introduced me as "One of the academy's own," a guest speaker with an "inspiring story."

I stood up. At the last minute, I grabbed my cane.

That I used my cane in front of the student body and faculty members was my biggest act of faith.

When Mrs. Curtis left, I wet my lips and folded up my cane. Then I adjusted the podium to give myself time to stop trembling. I looked over the audience and found my sister and her husband on one side of my niece. My mother sat on the other side, next to the aisle.

There couldn't have been more than thirty students attending. I recognized my Spanish students. My eyes rested on Piedad's lovely smile, which encouraged me. Most of the faculty members sat in the pew behind the students. Some smiled, some looked thoughtful. All seemed expectant.

I took a deep breath and began to speak. Soon, I lost my self-consciousness. My words tumbled out, one after the other.

"Do you know what a wonderful Lord we have?" I asked the students. "I'm just using myself as an example. But God doesn't play favorites. He loves all His children equally, and He knows what we want most. Listen to this! Our Heavenly Father allowed me to see *thirty-three* countries while I could still see well. I lived in *six*. Isn't that an incredible illustration of receiving blessings that are 'pressed down, shaken together and running over?'"

The room was silent, and I knew I had their attention. If only I could get the students' attention in the classroom like this.

"I'm sure that God gave me the desires of my heart because I trusted that He would provide the opportunities I needed. If we have even a little faith, He rewards us. The thing is, students, God doesn't always give our gifts in the wrapping we expect. So we need to observe, and yes, anticipate or we might miss them."

I craned my neck to see my mother. She had sacrificed her peace of mind so that I could follow my opportunities and receive the gifts prepared for me.

"God let me see the world, but not through the eyes I expected. I didn't want to run into little old Japanese ladies in the subway station. Neither did I want to fall down eighteen steps in Indonesia on my first day of work, nor did I want to get lost in Cairo because it turned dark sooner than I expected. But if I focused on all the accidents I encountered or might experience instead of the many friendships I made or the cultural aspects I learned about, I would have missed out on so many blessings."

I talked about how God builds our faith. "The thing is, nestled in that wrapped paper from God are lots of smaller gifts, for example, the fruit of the spirit. At first, we think we want that awesome, showy gift we envisioned, but once we start using the smaller gifts, they make us appreciate other aspects of life we never thought meant so much—both tangible and intangible, from our homes to our relationships."

I closed with my tribute to Bob and how he inspired me by his unflagging determination to prepare me for blindness from the start. "I hated the word 'blind,' and yet Bob showed me that it had no negative significance unless I chose to give it one." I explained how he modeled different approaches to handling the continuum of vision I lived with.

My final words came without being pre-planned. "Isn't that exactly what God does for us? We are invited to live for our Heavenly Father within a continuum of life experiences. We, ourselves, choose how to respond."

I carefully made my way down the stairs with my cane and sat down filled with wonder. I knew God gave me those final words to share. I hadn't rehearsed them; they just came to me at the moment I needed them. He also gave me the courage to pick up my cane and use it, which, at that moment, felt like the most frightening thing I had ever done.

After the talk, several students came up to investigate the visual aids I'd brought. I had my pillow and the alarm clock along with the sensor that shook the pillow. I set it and turned it on. "Put your hand on the pillow," I told one student.

A little bit of a ham, he chose to lay his head on the pillow. When the alarm went off, he jumped. "Wow! I don't think I want to use that kind of alarm. I don't want to feel that again," he said, rubbing his head as the others laughed.

"The funny thing is, you would use it again if you were deaf because it would wake you up," I said in instructor-mode. "You'd learn through experience that it wouldn't hurt you. Sometimes it just surprises you."

A parallel hit me immediately. That motion sensor is similar to how God sometimes wakes us up. We're often deaf to a typical alarm, but we respond immediately to the sensor. We may not like it or want to feel it again. But the more we wake up to it, the more we learn through past experiences that God doesn't want to hurt us. The surprise may even be such that it's worth waking up for.

That evening I found Mom seated in her reading chair, legs stretched out on the footstool. I shared the lesson I felt God had taught me with the alarm clock.

"You're really growing into a strong Christian. That was a good presentation today." She closed her book and smoothed the cover, flicking the top corner back and forth with her thumbnail in a nervous gesture, as if something was bothering her.

I started to thank her when she said pensively, "I wish your dad could have heard it."

Something in Mom's voice made me stop and look more closely at her. She appeared smaller, almost shrunken, in her fleece robe. What must run through her mind as I breezed by her, heading out the door or up to my apartment? She spent evenings reading her romance novels. Was she lonely?

My strong mother had rarely cried aside from when Dad died. She didn't want him to suffer, and when the pain grew too bad for him to bear, she'd prayed for God to take him. She preferred his peace over her loss.

I tried to think of something upbeat, but in the end, I just said, "Me, too."

She let out a long sigh. "I wish he could see you now."

I bit my lip. "He can, Mom." I leaned against the wall, one foot on top of the other. "Do you remember that wonderful treehouse Dad made for us when we were growing up? All the neighborhood kids used to come over and sleep in the treehouse? Remember the swings he made: the rope with a big knot in it and the tire swing that hung from the tree? I think we were the only family in our town, probably in the entire state of Pennsylvania, who could get down from a treehouse with a green fire pole. Mom, we had that gigantic slide that Dad fixed, and had to climb about twenty steps to get up there."

"He could build anything." Mom shifted her focus and a faraway look stole over her eyes. What was she thinking about? "The town supervisor gave that slide to your dad. The councilmen replaced the one in the park. It was the perfect height for that treehouse."

"Yeah, he made that small wooden platform, and we slid down from there. We used to slide down on waxed paper to go faster." I smiled at the memory.

"Your dad sure loved you kids," she said slowly, with a catch in her throat. I already knew what her next words would be. "They were some of the best years of our life. He said, 'We'd better enjoy them now because they grow up too darn fast.'"

And here I am, in my fifties all grown up.

"Mom, I'm sure he can see everything going on in our family. He's probably all stretched out in some great treehouse he built for himself there in heaven." I imagined what that would be like "Mom, I bet his vision is perfect."

We smiled at each other. I suppose we each found comfort in our memories. But more than that, we could be certain that we'd see Dad again one day.

I reminded myself to spend more time with Mom. My dad had it right. Time is precious. People leave us too darn fast.

As I crawled into bed that night, I thought about each gift God had provided for me, especially that beautiful moment with Mom at the end of the day.

Oh Lord, my cup runneth over.

Chapter 19
Back in the Classroom

Since I needed to administer only two final exams, my work load lightened, and I had ample time to complete my final grades.

Awards night came next. I had to present awards to the students with the highest grade point average in each of my Spanish classes.

"If you're not comfortable, perhaps one of the other teachers can present the awards for you," Mrs. Curtis suggested.

"No, no, I'll be fine. Are we going to present them in the chapel?"

"Yes, that's where we usually do it."

"I can do that." I could, couldn't I? Of course I could.

While I waited for my part in the awards program, I felt the old angst return. What if I tripped going up the steps? What if my eyes momentarily tricked me and part of the student was missing from my view? Did I just hold out the award and trust the student would see it?

I could hear Julio's voice in my head. *You're catastrophizing again.*

"…We move to high school foreign language awards."

Almost there. Almost there. Whew. Safe. I smiled at the crowd and opened up my manila folder to read the name on the first award.

As I leaned into the microphone to give some background information about the student, a terrible squelching sound erupted. I backed away. Something was wrong. The Math, or maybe it was the Social Studies, teacher came and tapped the microphone, switched it off and on before taking her seat on stage again. My second attempt sounded just as horrible. My heart thudded in my chest as I shoved the microphone away from me. *What was going on?*

I wiped my trembling, sweaty hands on my slacks and tried again, laughing nervously when the awful sound erupted again. With that cackle, I sounded like the wicked witch. Finally, I held the microphone several inches away and made my presentations. The audience probably couldn't hear me as well but the screeching stopped. I made it through my part and handed over the betraying steel wand to the next presenter. Red-faced, I took my seat on stage, fearing my legs would buckle under me any moment.

The next teacher had no problem whatsoever with the microphone. Her voice sounded clear and composed. Go figure. *Why did these strange things always happen to me?* As the program continued, my racing heart slowed down to its normal rhythm, and I relaxed.

The Math teacher came up to me afterward. "Don't worry about the microphone malfunction. It happens to all of us sooner or later," she consoled.

That night, Julio cleared up the mystery.

"Amy," he said, "Think about it. You know why it happened to you and not the teacher before or after you, don't you?"

"If I did, I certainly wouldn't be asking you," I snapped.

Julio groaned. "The microphone isn't alive, singling you out to throw a curse on you. It's not a personal attack." He laughed at me. "Haven't you figured it out yet? All that 'screeching,' as you call it, came from two little instruments called *hearing aids*."

"No way. Really?"

"Yes, really. My question is, why didn't you stop the program to tell your principal you had a problem? That's the logical course of action to follow. You don't need to be told that, do you?"

"I don't know, Julio." I sighed. "It never came to my mind. Tell you what, though, I'm never going to speak in public wearing my hearing aids again."

"Look at it this way. It's just another Amy predicament. You've had so many. What's one more?"

I laughed. "Oh, stop it."

"You see, I keep telling you not to lose your sense of humor."

"Well, it really didn't last all that long," I admitted. "But I would have never guessed the culprits were my hearing aids."

"Culprits? They're not alive either."

More laughter came, sweet and refreshing. Of course, I wasn't the only one to fight with a microphone. Other people laugh it off, and that's exactly what I should do, too.

God, I'm so thankful Julio reminds me to filter my circumstances through a lens of laughter.

The following Friday evening, our school held the graduation ceremony for the seniors with a reception afterward in the cafeteria. I sat down at a table with some of the faculty and made small talk. A teacher coughed. "Dry throat here. I hear a sparkling glass of punch calling my name."

"Me, too," I agreed, eying the table on the other side of the room.

"I'll get you one," she offered immediately. "Do you want a piece of cake while I'm up?"

I paused, uncertain of the best way to respond. Finally, I said, "Thanks so much. I need some exercise myself, though." I jumped up as if I had energy to run marathons.

"Here, hold onto my arm." She extended her arm, bent at the crook of her elbow.

I understood that she wanted to help me. She clearly had good intentions. But, for me, accepting help was new and a little unwelcome. I recalled how, as a toddler, my niece used to play with a wind-up wooden duck. She'd place it on the kitchen floor and watch it go, clapping her tiny hands when it ran into a chair or the leg of a table. She'd run and retrieve it for me to wind up again. Since my talk in the chapel, my colleagues were aware of my issues. Perhaps the faculty now viewed me as that wind-up duck. Maybe they thought if they didn't point me in the right direction or if they let me go, I'd run into something and spin my webbed feet.

I couldn't explain this to my colleague, of course, so I simply took her arm. We stopped to greet parents a few times on the way to the punch table. During those interludes, I had a strange desire to quack.

"How about this piece? Or would you like a corner slice? It has more frosting." Without waiting for my decision, she picked up the corner piece and steered me toward the punch bowl. She released my arm long enough to pour glasses of punch for both of us but took it again.

"Let me help," I offered, taking my glass of punch, leaving a splotchy trail way back to our table. I hoped no one saw that it was me. *Not a good duck!*

"There you go, m'dear," my colleague said, depositing me nicely beside the chair.

I sat down and took stock of my punch. Half a glass. I sloshed it around in the plastic cup and took a sip. *Still cold.* The ginger ale gave it a light bubbly flavor. With my finger, I stirred the dollop of melting sherbet, and took another sip. I picked up my fork and tasted a piece of the white cake. The corner piece had twice as much frosting on it. That was actually a good choice.

Suddenly, I recalled the trail of punch leading "home." Craning my neck, I strained to see how incriminating it might be. By now, feet had trampled and fanned it out. I covered my mouth and giggled when I realized it looked a lot like a duck actually walked through it with its webbed feet. "Quack. Quack," I whispered to myself.

The teachers chatted together while I sat quietly in their midst. Would I ever feel like one of them? Or would my differences always set me apart?

When I unfolded my cane and stood up to leave, my colleagues barely noticed. Slipping away from the table, I found Mrs. Curtis and thanked her for the lovely celebration. Before she could respond, a parent launched into conversation. With a quick wave, I left the bright red punch along with the sheet cake covered in red and blue flowers behind.

I took a deep breath and stepped through the faculty door for the last time that year. I lived only a few blocks away, and the darkness would test my new cane skills. I had not yet used my cane at night.

With the meager light shining from the street lamp, I oriented myself to the street facing the school. I mentally reviewed the directions. Turn to the left. Walk four blocks. Find the big library at the corner. Cross the street. Walk five blocks. You should be on your own street. Cross it and find the sidewalk. To your right is the street beside your house. Cross that and you're home.

The darkness seemed to swallow me as I inched steadily forward. I swept my cane in front of me, keeping myself centered on the sidewalk.

Stay positive, I admonished myself. I was getting there. I was doing it. Keep on going.

I visualized the environment—so familiar in the daylight and yet so unfamiliar in the dark. *Listen for traffic cues.* My confidence grew until I came upon the barking dog. I mentally went through the location of each house. If my memory served me right, the dog shouldn't be on the right-hand side. He should be on the left. The growling disoriented me.

How close is he to me? *Where am I going?* Did I make the right turns? Could this be a wrong neighborhood? Is he on a leash? The thoughts tumbled through my head. Did I have my cell phone? I might have to call my brother.

I frantically tried to remember what Bob told me to do when I get lost.

Take a step back and explore my environment with my cane. Bob emphasized the next step: I needed to reorient myself in whatever way I could.

I recalled something in the Bible about standing at a crossroads and looking—no, *asking*—for "the good way." What did it say? Go that good way? Walk in it? And we will find … what? Rest? Peace? In my situation, would I find my way home? The key was in asking. *Where is that good way, God?*

The dog continued to bark. I stood still and listened. Suddenly, I remembered that on the corner of Frick and Hathaway, there lived a dog in a fenced-in yard. If that was the dog, I needed to retrace my steps to return to Hathaway, and turn left. Then I would arrive home. I wouldn't be lost anymore. Maybe I wouldn't have to call my brother, after all.

I straightened up and moved hesitantly until I arrived at Hathaway Street. I made the turn and used my cane to ensure that I stayed in the center of the sidewalk. As I continued to step forward in the darkness, I swept through my doubts and fears. I realized I could trust my cane.

Hallelujah! I saw a light exactly where it should be, shining from behind our living room curtains. I had made it home.

God, how is it that the words to that scripture came to me at the exact point I needed it? You are supplying my needs in a crazy, exciting way! I need to find that scripture. I flipped the pages to my Bible and skimmed the highlighted passages but I couldn't find anything that resembled those special words.

I needed a break. I absently picked up my cell phone. Lisa. I would talk to Lisa. She might even know the scripture I was looking for.

We chatted for awhile, and then she told me about a scripture on her heart.

This was not unusual. Lisa often texted or shared scriptures with me. I jotted the reference down. But I didn't need to wait to look it up. She read it to me over the phone. I'd been resting my face on my hand but when I heard her words, I sat up straight.

"Lisa! I think that's the scripture that came to mind earlier when I was lost. God was speaking to me in my situation. Now you've confirmed it."

"Glory to God," she whispered. "The passage is so beautiful. I was meant to share that with you."

"Yes!"

After we hung up, I thought about how God works in our lives. He is in the business of reorienting people. When we go down the wrong road in our spiritual darkness, something stops us, the way the barking dog stopped me. Whenever something doesn't feel right, when we ask Him for directions, He backs us up and reorients us.

God was growing my faith, I realized. When I overcame my difficulties, I trusted Him a little bit more each time. He was using these scary situations to reorient me to Him.

I went to my Bible and highlighted the passage in yellow, marking the date next to it.

This is what the Lord says: Stand at the crossroads
And look; ask for the ancient paths and where the
good way is, and walk in it and you will find rest.

Jeremiah 6:16, NIV.

Curled up in bed that night, I envisioned myself as maybe God had confused and disoriented in my own neighborhood. But maybe He wanted to teach me a life lesson.

Maybe He was saying, *I know you're confused right now. You're defensive around others. You want to prove you are self-reliant. I understand all this. Reorient yourself to Me. I will show you the good way, and you will find rest in your life situation. Rely on Me like you're learning to rely on your cane.*

That day, my school year had officially ended. For some reason, God often chose milestone days in which to teach me life lessons.

Chapter 20
HOW TO MISS A PICNIC

Mom, the official mail-sorter in the family, called me down to the living room. "Looks like something came from the college where you taught. Open it up, so I can see what it says."

I laughed. That was Mom, nosy as ever. Curious, I tore open the envelope. Swatting at a pesky fly, which had somehow made its way into the house, I unfolded the crisp letter and started to read. "Oh! The college offered me another teaching contract for the Asian Studies course this coming fall." I clapped my hands, creasing the letter sandwiched between them. "I can't believe they asked me to teach again after all the difficulties I had. Wow!"

Mom settled back down in her chair, carefully leaning her cane against the wicker armrest. "Isn't that something? But you shouldn't be surprised," she said, reaching for the letter. I could tell she couldn't wait to read the words for herself. "You're a good teacher. I don't know how much time you put into your classes, but you were always at the computer writing your lectures."

"Yeah." I always over-prepared. So I took the disappointments that much harder. But now it seemed I needn't have worried. I had my second job again.

When I called the director, Annabelle Sparks, to tell her I would accept the position, her voice sounded muffled and I heard her shuffling papers. "Hang on a sec." I heard her say, "Be sure to address it to all incoming freshmen."

Annabelle returned to the phone. "Sorry, we're trying to finish up the details to our Orientation program. You *know* how that is." She let out a big sigh. "Just return the contract in the mail in the morning. Classes don't start until late August. I wrote a start date on the contract, didn't I?"

"Yes, it's included. I'll mail it out first thing."

I zipped up my purse and left the bank, catching my cell phone on the second ring. "Julio, guess what I received?"

"A get-out-of-jail key?"

"Ha ha. I got a new contract to teach the Asian Studies course this fall." I couldn't keep the excitement out of my voice.

"Really? You'd better make the changes to your syllabus early this time," he warned.

"Well, I have a couple of months." Julio always rushed me.

"You know how you always wait until the last minute and then get stressed." He had a point. "And if I were you, I'd telephone the one in charge of the course at the main campus and liaise to find out the topics the instructor focuses on and which book is used there. Don't leave anything to chance."

"I well, that's a good idea." I'd never think of doing that on my own.

On my bank receipt I wrote, CALL MAIN CAMPUS. LIAISE.

That afternoon I followed up with the instructor, an adjunct professor, who had a Japanese accent. "I'll be happy to talk with you about how I teach the course," Mrs. Tanaka offered politely. It was difficult to tell if she meant it or not. She had a certain distant tone in her voice that I recognized from my time in Japan. People always came across as extremely polite, but that didn't necessarily indicate they meant what they said. As long as they spoke kindly, they didn't lose face.

I needed a certain "in" to discover if she really planned to help me.

"*Daijobu.*" Okay.

Mrs. Tanaka sounded surprised. "You can speak Japanese?"

"*Hai, sukoshi, Tanaka-san.*" Yes, a little. "I took some courses in Japanese at the University of Maryland. But a long time ago."

"*Yoi desu.*" Excellent. "You can call me Hitomi or Hitomi-san."

I smiled. Sharing a common language always seemed to break the ice. For a few minutes, we compared notes about Japanese cities we both knew. I asked her how long she had lived in the United States.

"A long time. But I return every few years so I don't forget my roots."

Finally, Hitomi-san ended the phone conversation with an invitation. "There's a group of Asia-Pacific professionals who join together for a picnic at Presque Isle, you know, on the peninsula? Would you like to meet them? I can formally introduce you there if you'd like."

"You bet!"

"I'll send you some information about the gathering and meet you at the picnic. We can proceed from there," she promised in her lightly-accented speech. "It'll be an excellent networking tool. Maybe you can even find some guest speakers to enhance your course material."

"That would be great!"

In the back of my mind, I imagined getting several members of the Asian community on board to form a pool of resources the students could interview. Julio had told me he required his students in the Chicano Studies program at San Diego State to interview someone of that background and prepare a presentation on what they learned. I planned to do the same. I couldn't wait to tell Julio about my new contacts.

The only hindrance to carrying out my plan was transportation. Since

I didn't drive, I had to find a reliable driver. The way I saw it, the success of my second Asian Studies course hinged on this one critical day of networking.

Lisa, one of the few people I could call on for a project like this, quickly volunteered. "Whatever you need, I'm there for you. I'll be your driver. Gimme a picnic and I'll show up."

"Of course, you're invited. Asia-Pacific Picnic, here we come!"

The picnic started at noon. Dressed and ready to go at ten o'clock, I drummed my fingers on the table and read the flyer again. I had made some jelly-filled cookies to take along with me as my contribution. Placing them on a paper plate, I covered it with cellophane. When I finished, there was nothing else to do but wait for Lisa. I willed the hands of the clock to move ahead. Finally, the time arrived ... but my ride didn't.

"Be patient," I scolded myself. "She'll be here soon." She had to be. She knew that I needed to network so that the local Asians would be interested in meeting my students.

The time dragged on. Where could she be? Why wasn't she answering her cell phone? *Please, God. Don't let her forget.*

At around two o'clock, Lisa rang me. "I'm on my way."

"Sure. No problem." Did I sound cheery enough? She was still my ride. Anyway, we had a couple of hours left.

Five miles down the road, Lisa announced, "We just need to make one quick stop."

What? I gritted my teeth and re-calculated the time. *Not good.* It would take thirty minutes to get to the beach from home even without an extra stop, but we could *still* make it. I hoped. "Oh. Really? Where?"

"These darn bugs!" She seemed excessively preoccupied with squirting windshield wiper fluid onto the glass and flipping on the wipers.

Neither of us spoke until we arrived at her destination.

Office Depot. Come on! How is this necessary?

"I'll be right out," she promised. Whatever she needed couldn't wait until later. Apparently. I couldn't believe I was waiting yet again for her.

At last we arrived at Presque Isle. One long road circled the peninsula and, as usual, traffic was backed up even though it had rained hard on the way in. Nothing slowed the tourists down in summer. "So, Lisa, where is Beach 11?" I tried to keep my voice nonchalant.

She grimaced. "I'm not sure. But we'll find it," she added reassuringly.

If we did, it wouldn't be any time soon. We drove and drove. As the minutes ticked by, my chest started to feel tight. Hitomi-san was such a good contact. She could help me interest the others in my project.

Tick! Tick!

Lisa maneuvered the car into a tight parking spot and switched the car off. "How about if we get out here and ask?" She pointed to a building. "There's a First Aid Station. I'll ask there. You go ask those picnickers."

Barefooted, Lisa awkwardly made her way over the gravel to a crude brick building. The sun was out now, and from the looks of it, the hot gravel was scorching her toes. What happened to Lisa's shoes?

Did Lisa even bring her shoes? I couldn't remember if she wore any into the store or not. But I wasn't paying attention to her feet then. I was looking at my watch. Knowing Lisa, she heard me ask her to the "beach" and that was all she cared about. She never thought of any other place or the need for shoes. That was Lisa. We were never going to make it! And I realized as I got out that I had left my cane at home. I still held the plate of cookies in my hand and the cling wrap now stuck to the jelly. Why didn't I leave the cookies in the car?

I hurried over to the picnickers. "Do you know where Beach 11 is?"

The man in the group, the one I assumed to be the dad, shrugged. "We're between Beach Six and Seven. Not sure about Beach 11. Your guess is as good as mine."

I gulped. It could be miles. *Oh Lord, help us make it! Where is Lisa?* Finally, I saw her. She tiptoed back across the parking area. "I guess it's back a ways," she reported, making a face.

I couldn't help myself and blurted out, "I've been looking forward to this networking opportunity for days. I thought you knew where Beach 11 was. Or at least you led me to believe you did. We are so late."

"Okay, I don't have any shoes. You go and try to make it." Lisa pushed me toward the sidewalk. "GO!"

"What? No, let's stay together."

"I hate to say this, but not only did I not bring any shoes, I'm also out of gas. Either way, I'll slow you down." She snapped her fingers as if she had an idea. "Give me the money for the gas, and I'll get it so we won't run out."

I wanted to slap her. Let's get this straight. I'm half-blind. I forgot my cane. And you expect me to go walking miles—by myself—carrying this flimsy plate of jelly cookies to try to find Beach 11, and any picnickers that might still be there. I don't think so.

"Go," she urged. "No, wait. First the money...."

I glared daggers. She appeared not to notice. At an impasse, I reached into my pocket and took out a five-dollar-bill.

She grabbed the money. "Okay, now. Go!" She rushed—as much as a bare-footed woman could rush on a sun-scorched pavement–to her car to get gas.

I marched in the opposite direction. That Lisa! How could she almost run out of gas, take my money and make *me* walk on my important Asia-Pacific networking day? Why didn't she ask me for gas when we left the house? She had promised to help me. But no, she didn't even have the sense to bring any shoes. The longer I walked, the longer the list of Lisa's idiosyncrasies grew. Like a Catch-22, the more I dwelled on what was sure to be a lost opportunity, the angrier I became. I moved faster. Stepped higher. Stomped harder. After awhile, smoldering anger consumed me.

I never saw the tree branch dangling over the walkway. The leafy branch, still wet and dripping from the afternoon rain shower, slapped me in the face. I reeled, disoriented and lost among the dark leaves blocking my vision. As I battled my way back to sunlight, my purse, which dangled off my elbow, snagged in the leaves. It pulled my arm down and trapped it, too.

I should have known my situation could only get worse.

While trying to free my arm, I forced the tip of the branch out of my way to retrieve my purse. When I released the branch, it snapped back as if it were a slingshot, shooting a mass of leaves in my direction. When they slammed against me, I stumbled and my other arm hit the trunk of the tree causing my plate of cookies to slide out of my hand. I dashed forward to save them and fell. My right foot landed directly on the plate of cookies, smashing them into tiny fragments that crumbled off the plate and onto the cement.

I fell silent. My eyes traveled slowly over the disaster scene.

It figured! Served me right, too. When I was carried away with my emotions, the tree branch slugged me, and I ended up with a trail of broken cookies stuck to the bottom of my shoe. I felt like a circus clown.

When others feel angry, they seem to let loose. But with my impeding blindness, my vision always interferes, and I have egg on my face, or, in this case, cookies crumbling around my feet. Why in the world do I put myself into these situations when I'm carrying something—and that something is not a cane?

Laughter bubbled out of me as I sat on my bum in my wet Bermuda shorts. I looked like I'd been through a war with the broken leaves, twigs and cookies surrounding me. People stared as they gave me a wide berth. They probably wondered what on earth had happened. I didn't think about it until later but no one even offered to help me up. I probably looked too far beyond help. *Oh God, thank you for the sunshine today. Thank you for sturdy shoes, two good feet to walk with, and yes, for trees to slap the silly out of me. I even thank you for my limited vision because I sure didn't see this day coming. But You always help me get through these situations.* I giggled. *That'll teach me. Next time I'll remember my cane.*

When I looked down at my arm, I realized my watch was gone. Had I lost it during the fall?

I saw a jogger pass by. "What time is it?"

"Four-thirty," he shouted back.

Who could I line up for my Asian Studies class now? I let out a big sigh. What a crazy disastrous day! I *wanted* to feel the injustice. But when I recalled the branch, which in my mind's eye, seemed almost human in its attack on me, truly, I couldn't stop laughing.

As I continued to walk, I grew pensive. I thought about my response, not only on that day, but in general. I hated confrontation. I realized that I rarely, if ever, confronted the person who caused my anger. Maybe I'd picked up some Japanese traits when I lived there. As a culture, the Japanese dislike confrontation. I responded afterward, usually when I was alone. That day I'd stomped my feet like a child having a tantrum, taking it out on my environment—and didn't stop until my environment fought back.

How would our day have gone if I had been honest about how much this day meant to me? Should we have talked it out more in advance? What if I had communicated to Lisa how upset I was with her late arrival and the extra stop? Would we have then have arrived in time?

A horn beeped.

I looked up to see Lisa at the wheel. At least she hadn't abandoned me. My anger dissolved. Instead, I saw only my close friend who'd pitched in to take me to a picnic.

Lisa rolled down her window and called out, "Are we too late?"

"Yeah, I'm afraid so. Did you get the gas?"

"Enough to make it home. Amy, we sure know how to miss a picnic, don't we? I really wanted you to make it."

I turned sideways and looked at her. We? Lisa seemed so dejected that I found myself comforting her. "It's all right, Lisa. If it's in God's plan for me to have a guest speaker, He will make that connection." I sighed. "He's made all sorts of life-changing connections for me—and that includes our friendship."

"Oh, yes!" Lisa took her hand off the steering wheel and high-fived me. "Remember when we ran into each other at the garage sale? I was thrilled when I found out you'd moved back home, too. We've been friends for…what? More than twenty years. You're not only a dear friend, you're my sister in Christ and my prayer bud! Love you, girl!"

Wouldn't you know, on my grumpiest day, she turned around and showered me with compliments! That's Lisa. What would I do without her? *Thank you, God. You not only share laughter with me through my frequent and absurd calamities, You use them to purposefully turn me toward You. This way, I can't miss Your hand in my life. Blind or not, I can still see You clearly. And You always provide the right connections. So I have to trust that whatever resources You provide for this course will be what You want me to use.*

My stomach growled as Lisa pulled into my driveway. She let her sporty red Ford Escort idle. "Amy, I know you really wanted to make the picnic." She gathered some pebbles from the floor mat in front of her seat and tossed them out the window. "But why was it so important to you? Is this something to do with your hearing or vision?"

"No, not at all." I rolled up my beach towel and held out a hand for my purse that Lisa handed to me from the floor. "I just wanted to make my class more interesting. You know, improve some of my activities."

"Sorry I screwed you up." She looked contrite. "One of those days, I guess."

"Forget it." I suddenly realized it didn't matter and waved away any importance it had. "Chances are, you and I are going to look back on today and laugh, making it one of those "do-you-remember-when days.""

She brightened. "Yeah, one of our *Thelma and Louise* adventures."

We both took a quiet moment to savor our friendship, one that allowed loyalty and laughter to overcome the petty irritations that arose when we didn't communicate well or understand each other.

"Love you, girl!" She tugged on the seatbelt and buckled it. "I gotta get going. Bitsy is waiting to eat. Gimme a call whenever."

I grinned. Someone, or in this case, a dog, was always waiting on her.

"See you!" I called, and waved goodbye as she backed out.

As I turned the key and let myself into the apartment, I wondered if I had been a hundred percent truthful with Lisa, or even to myself about the purpose for my networking. Was my search for native Asian guest speakers really an attempt to have students overlook any vision or hearing mistakes I might make in the coming term?

That I might have an underlying agenda made me feel uneasy.

My challenges weren't going to disappear just because I had a second chance at teaching the course. I couldn't imagine myself using my cane in the classroom when I taught. Also, my hearing aids didn't solve all my hearing problems.

That's why God was providing this intensive training course for me. I'd be able to ask experts how to better handle these situations. The training sounded better all the time!

CHAPTER 21
TAKING THE NEXT STEP

Everywhere I looked, I saw long red and white canes similar to mine. Some were folded up and stored under the picnic table, others leaned against the bench. I glimpsed a couple beside the door frame leading into Bob's house. More canes stayed with their owners, who unconsciously twirled them between their fingers, rocked them back and forth, or periodically folded and unfolded them as they conversed. From all appearances, these canes seemed to have become an extension of the people who used them.

Having so many canes around me made me nervous.

I'd never been to a function with only (or mostly) blind people in attendance. These canes were blatant reminders of my own vision impairment, something I still had difficulty accepting. More often than not, I "forgot" to carry my cane unless someone or something brought it to my attention.

Today's picnic at Bob's place had forced me to take it out from under my bed, brush off the dust and use it again. I felt a little guilty that once the school year ended, I had stopped using it. I hadn't even had a mobility lesson with Bob for over a month. Without my accountability partners, I became lazy and reverted to walking with my head down as I sought out obstacles in time to prevent an accident. I obviously suffered from a conflicting love / hate relationship with my cane and felt some kind of sensory overload.

If I took away the canes and simply looked at the little flags centered on the tables that were decorated with red, white and blue napkins, I could be anywhere enjoying this picnic.

But the prospect of maneuvering around the tables in such close quarters seemed daunting. Was I up to the task? What if my cane accidentally collided with someone else's? In my mind, I could already hear the sounds of the canes coming to blows. Hundreds of swords clashing—a free-for-all where someone would end up impaled by my cane.

With an imagination like this, was it any wonder I was leery of leaving my seat? Even little mishaps made me uneasy. What if I stepped on someone's heels? What if, when I unfolded my cane, it sprang out and hit someone in the head? That had happened once. In fact, the tip of my cane had knocked off a woman's glasses! I convinced myself that I was a danger to other vision-impaired people and shouldn't enjoy this picnic at all.

But when Bob's wife said, "Come on, Amy, eat up," I hadn't the heart to refuse. I limited myself to my favorites—baked beans, a burger, and salt-and-vinegar chips—with a glass containing some kind of patriotic red, white and blue beverage. No seconds for me.

The canes didn't worry my brother. He loaded up his plate a couple of times and seemed at ease with our host and the other guests. While Mike squeezed mustard onto his hotdog, he said "Bob, are you a Seawolves fan?"

"I do enjoy a good ballgame," he said, biting into a chip. "My wife and I purchase tickets to the Jerry Uht Stadium when we can. The team isn't bad for semi-pros."

I wondered how Bob "saw" the game. When he listened to the announcer's blow-by-blow narration, did it create enough of a picture in his mind? Or did his wife supplement it? I'll bet she never grabbed his arm and said, "Did you see that home run?" Something I'm sure I would have done.

The two talked baseball for awhile. They admired some of the better players who had been transferred to the major league parent team, the Detroit Tigers, and, of course, compared notes on the last few games. When Bob stood up to circulate among the other guests, Mike offered him an official Seawolves' foul ball, one of the many he caught outside the stadium.

"I'll get the baseball before I go. It's in my car. Would you like to go to a game sometime? I could pick you up. I usually get free tickets when I eat at Wendy's or McDonalds, so I can pick up an extra one."

"That would certainly be do-able." Bob nodded a couple of times. "But give me some notice, Michael. I'm not much on spur-of-the-moment engagements."

"Yeah, I could do that," my brother said eagerly. "But I need your phone number. Or maybe I can get it from my sister."

When they agreed to meet, I savored the moment as if it were a sweet slice of watermelon. My brother, normally quiet except when it came to baseball, didn't reach out often. Bob, outgoing as he was, still had that quirky formality about him. I loved it that he even referred to the baseball stadium by its proper name. Bob and my brother were probably opposites except when it came to their love for baseball.

Still elated over Mike's invitation to Bob, I caught the tail end of a conversation about Braille and turned to the woman next to me. She was talking about Braille to the next person over. "Excuse me, do you read Braille?"

Startled, she turned toward me. "Yes, I do."

"Me, too!"

"Are you proficient?" she inquired.

"Oh no, no, nothing like that. I just started learning how to read and write. Well, I only wrote once," I admitted. "And that came out backwards."

"I'll bet you were using a slate and stylus, weren't you?"

"Yes." I laughed. "I'm told that it's a common mistake when you're new to Braille."

The woman took a sip of her diet cola. "I suppose. We all go through it. Like a rite of initiation." When we both laughed, it also felt like a rite of passage.

"I've been reading practically forever," she said draping a sweater around her shoulders. "These days, the young people want to do everything with technology. What if these websites and the talking books and what-have-you break down? Where will they be then, huh?" She shook her head sadly. "Nothing can replace Braille."

"That's for sure," I said, as if I were an expert.

I didn't know that Braille was on its way out. It seemed as if there were two camps: those that valued the skills and those who rejected them. It fascinated me because I viewed learning Braille as mastering another language. Of course, proponents feel that people who know Braille are more self-reliant. This is exactly how I would approach a new culture. I wouldn't want to depend on any one thing in order to move forward.

Bob was the perfect host—casual, humorous, and efficient. Between him and his sighted wife, the picnic ran smoothly.

"Have you met Stanley yet?" Bob asked in passing. "Stan, let me introduce Amy to you. She's considering seeking admittance to my alma mater, the Louisiana Center for the Blind." He dusted off his hands as if he had done his job well.

I bit my thumbnail and blurted out, "Uh, Bob, now I'm not sure about that.

I might end up at the Cleveland Sight Center."

"The Sight Center!" He made a face. "What happened to change your mind?"

"Well, I haven't completely decided," I hedged. "But it's closer to home."

"The problem is their emphasis," Bob explained. "The 'Sight' Center implies doing whatever you can to save what you will eventually lose. What good is that? You need to learn how to cope with being blind, hence, the name and intensified emphasis at the Louisiana School for the Blind."

I still didn't understand the problem, as long as I received intensive life skills training.

Stanley shook his head. "She's in denial." He shrugged as if he didn't know what else to say or do. He was probably joking. But I didn't know what he meant, so I thought it best to change the subject. I cleared my throat. "What great weather! Will there be fireworks tonight?"

It appeared that emotional fireworks had started already.

My supposed denial began a debate about what constituted correct terminology among the blind. Both *blind* and *sight* acted as "trigger" words, igniting people's passions. From what I could glean, some considered "sight" a cover-up, and "blind" as acceptance of one's situation. This extended to training centers and their training philosophies, which hinged on their names.

"What's wrong with saying *sight*? At least you're using what you have," grumbled the lady next to me. She patted my hand, as if to comfort me and whispered, "Stick with your choice."

Stanley objected. "It's a philosophy. A *false* philosophy. That's the problem."

The argument turned both political and personal. I couldn't believe how my innocent comment to Bob caused so many hard feelings. I felt as if I had entered a foreign country without knowing the rules or the culture—and had just committed a serious *faux pas*.

Bob's wife rapped the table with a container of cling-wrap. "Come on, folks. Lighten up. It's a holiday in the land of the free and home of the brave. We don't have a permit for these kinds of fireworks."

I sat quietly eating at the end of one table. I hated to admit it but I eavesdropped on a conversation at the picnic table across from me. A young, slightly overweight twenty-something woman was saying to the man next to her, "Do you have more blind or sighted friends?"

"No contest. I have more blind friends. Sighted people just don't get how difficult it is."

She sighed. "I know. They're like, 'Come on, let's go here, let's go there.' They're clueless about the obstacles we face."

I tried not to take their comments to heart. They didn't know I considered myself "sighted." It wasn't as if Bob had said, "Hey everyone, meet Amy, she can see." I was pretty certain that several of the guests had different levels of vision, not just me.

If the two people at the other table ever saw me in a different environment and without my cane, would they assume I had no clue? Was that the way I felt about the students and faculty members at the school? I hoped not. It seemed so close-minded. I had a feeling that lots of people wanted to help, and be friendly but were afraid of saying or doing the wrong thing. It wasn't a matter of not getting it.

I heard a cough and looked up. "Wait a minute. Even if people seem clueless, how can they understand if we don't communicate openly about our needs and what it's like?" It was the same woman who had objected in the last argument. She seemed bent on playing the devil's advocate. "I think it's our job to educate them."

Did I need to be educated? Was I uncouth? I wanted to say, "I have a Master's Degree. Do I need more education?" but, of course, I knew that wasn't what she meant.

She went on. "What does it matter if people are sighted or blind? We need to make friends with both. Personally, I have a lot of well-meaning sighted friends who help me all the time."

Their conversation intrigued me. I looked at those around me and wondered what I had in common with them—other than the obvious vision impairment. Was that the only basis for establishing friendships that I had to look forward to? Or would I stick with my sighted friends?

Of course, almost everyone I knew could see, or maybe I should say, see *well*, just like I used to.

Restless, I clattered down the steps in my loose-fitting sandals. Not much to see except for the rose bushes. Who pruned them? Was it Bob or his wife? I wouldn't be surprised if Bob had done it himself. He accomplished more blind than most sighted people did. I bent over to touch the soft red petals. The scent of roses always reminded me of my father, who used to cultivate them in our back yard. I wandered back to the house, found an empty lawn chair next to the bottom of the steps, and sat down.

Shortly after that, an olive-skinned young man eased into a chair not far from mine. He wore dark mirror glasses, a polo shirt with a zippered jacket over it, blue jeans, and black dress shoes. His clothing looked a little formal for a picnic. I saw him pull out his cell phone and speak into it. Was it voice activated? He waited several seconds and then said, "Hey, whattaya doin', dude?" Voice activated.

I recognized his Middle-Eastern accent even though he seemed to have the slang down. He stretched his legs and settled in for a long conversation. Finally, he finished.

"Hi," I called over. "Are you one of Bob's client's, too?"

"Yeah, I've gone out a couple of times with him," he said casually. "It's just a formality. I taught myself how to get around a *long* time ago."

"Really?"

"I just moved to this area. I'm transferring into EUP—Edinboro University of Pennsylvania—for the fall term. I got involved with the Bureau of Blindness where I met Bob—'cuz they'd kinda help cover some of my expenses."

I lifted an eyebrow. Knowing where to seek out resources is the key for everyone, not just college students. "Oh, yeah."

He shrugged and held out his hand. "My name's Moe, that's with an 'e.'"

"I can tell by your accent that's not your real name, is it? *Assalam Alekum, teman.*"

He didn't look all that surprised to hear my Arabic greeting "*Teman,* what's that?" He gave me a blank look.

"Isn't *teman* Arabic for friend?"

"No," he said enjoying my confusion.

When I finally realized that I was speaking Indonesian, I rolled my eyes. What was it in Arabic? *Sedik?* I explained what happened and corrected myself. "Unfortunately, sometimes my different languages interfere with each other." His laughter broke the ice between us.

"To go back to your name…" I was sure of myself on this one. "You've Americanized it, right? Is it Mohamed?"

"You're good." He laughed again, flipping his cell phone in his hand. "I go by Moe. What about you, Miss Indonesia?"

"I'm Amy. Hey, we both have three-letter first names."

"Huh?"

"Our names. They both have only three letters. That's kind of neat. So where are you from?"

"Abu Dhabi," he said casually, texting.

"Really? I lived for nine years in the Emirates. I came back to the States three years ago." I switched to Arabic again, asking him where he lived in the capital city.

"That's Egyptian Arabic," he observed without answering my question. He seemed to lose interest. "I speak a little Arabic but don't understand much. I hated the Emirates. I never want to live there again."

I brushed away a bee circling my drink. "Were you born there?"

"No. I was born in Iraq. But at age six or seven, I was adopted by a rich Emirati family," he said scornfully. "My 'mother' is angry with me. Last year they wanted me to marry a local girl. I didn't want anything to do with arranged marriages. Or with Islam. I'm an atheist," he declared, jabbing at the small keyboard on his cell phone.

"Hmm. Many of my students had arranged marriages, and they were unhappy as well."

He jutted out his top lip and swore. He really didn't like it.

Moe was not a typical Emirati in the least. The men rarely refused marriage, and none I knew would dare to cast off their religion. Islam was such a big deal in any Arab culture that to reject it publicly, well, he could be killed for it. Besides, religion and culture were intertwined. I was beginning to understand some of his conflict and why he spoke so harshly of his life back in the Middle East. Also, why he was living in the United States.

But my curiosity was piqued. "How did you happen to get adopted by an Emirati family if you were born in Iraq?"

He slid the keyboard shut and tossed his phone into his jacket pocket.

"When I was three, I was walking down the street with my real mom. A roadside bomb blew up in my face. Later, I woke up in a hospital. I got blinded," he said matter-of-factly. "No one could find my mom. Either she didn't survive or didn't want me."

"Wow," I said, sympathizing.

"Anyway, I had to go to an orphanage. But no one knew what to do with a blind kid. After awhile, the director learned about a family with the mom in the Diplomatic Corps and asked her to adopt me." He smirked and then added, "More likely to get me out and make his life easier. End of story."

"Wow. I'm so sorry." I paused, trying to think of something positive to say. "Your English is very good."

He fidgeted for a moment. "As I said, I speak more English than Arabic. What about you? What did you do in the Emirates?"

As I opened up about my life in the Middle East, I realized that people seek common experiences in starting friendships. I liked meeting Moe. We shared real interests and knew about the same culture and traditions. What was even better, except for explaining how he came to live in the Emirates, he never talked about his sight or asked me about mine.

It somehow felt...liberating.

I wondered if Bob felt the same sense of liberation. Or perhaps he never felt that fear.

Losing my sight gradually meant constantly adapting to new limits and finding ways to either be comfortable with the changes or overcome them. Either course of action means I had fewer choices. But that afternoon, I discovered that I could always choose my own friends, just like other blind people could choose their friendships based on individual preferences. That would never be taken away.

In my case, I loved meeting people from other countries. As far as I knew, only one foreigner had attended Bob's picnic, and God made sure I met him. It seems to me that God wanted to ease me into the foreign "country" of canes and blindness, and the best way to do that was to put me in an atmosphere of comfort. It tickled me when I realized that level of comfort came from meeting someone from a real foreign country.

God delights in turning the tables on His children. I love His humor.

Chapter 22
STREET SMARTS

"Ready for the challenge? You're going to wear your sleep shades from start to finish."

I tried to ignore the excitement in my trainer's voice. *What had I gotten myself into?* This time I had to pool all my skills and cross hectic city streets to find a couple of addresses that only Bob knew, then eat in a restaurant, all while wearing my sleep shades.

Bob twirled me around as if I were playing pin-the-tail-on-the-donkey. "Now, make your way to the back passenger car door." He waited for me to reach it. "Are you there yet?"

I rolled my eyes. "Yes."

"All right, you are now permitted to enter the van."

I saluted in the direction of his voice, glad that he couldn't see me, and felt for the door handle to ease myself in. At the time, I could not understand why Bob felt the need to keep me in such secrecy. I already had a poor sense of direction, even when nothing physical obstructed my vision. I suppose he wanted to challenge me so that I would receive the maximum benefit from his training. Although I had come a long way from my early

150

training, I still had many lessons to learn.

"I'm going to give you some time to warm up. I won't just throw you into the situation," he explained.

"Warming up would be letting me see before getting into the van," I complained.

His usually-pleasant voice hardened. "You already know how to see. You've been doing that all your life. You are learning how to get around by *not* seeing. I will not be happy if you lose your vision before you are sufficiently prepared. I'm teaching you how to be…."

"I know. *Blind!*" I bit off the word.

Bob continued calmly, "I was going to say 'self-sufficient.'"

Leaning back into the vinyl seat, I exhaled and tried to calm down. Why had I started out in attack mode? Why was I so sensitive?

I knew the answer—The Accuser. The joy-stealer. Satan. He was trying to block my focus by placing my fears and insecurities in front of me. He'd like nothing better than to cut me off from the confidence I had developed and prevent what Christ could do through me.

No way. He wasn't going to win this one. God was going to work in and through me this afternoon and show me that together Bob and I could accomplish what I never dreamed we could.

I could almost hear Satan's rebuttal: *You think you're tough but you're just vain. You couldn't do any of this stuff on your own. You need Bob to chase after you to keep you from any kind of injury. Fake progress.*

I didn't even bother to answer his lies.

I noticed the heavy paper in my lap, and then I remembered that I'd brought the Braille practice sheet with me. "Hey Bob, I did more practice in Braille. You want to see what I've done?"

"You remembered to re-do it," he approved. "Let me read it and see what progress you've achieved."

I handed him the paper.

"Well done," he stated a few minutes later. "Ah, this is the poem you mentioned." He read it silently without commenting. I felt goose bumps prickle on my arms. Would he understand this had to do with my vision loss and how God picked me up when I fell? Or maybe I would have to explain. Give my testimony.

I felt the edge of the paper as he handed it back to me. "You're a writer," he said. "It's full of imagery. I don't know anyone who started out writing poetry in the initial phases of learning Braille."

"Well, I couldn't give it the same written structure in Braille as I did on the computer." I smoothed the paper out. "But I hope the message came through."

"Indeed. You're an optimist. The title says it all, 'Perfumed Dreams.'"

"But...." I felt God telling me to wait and instead, asked Bob about what he thought I should expect from the more intensive mobility training I was considering and followed up with another, more pressing question. "Are you sure the Bureau of Blindness will pay for it?" I didn't have any money.

"Certainly, they will," he assured me. "The State of Pennsylvania has quite a bit of money tucked away for such things. Our clients don't know to tap into that unless we explicitly tell them."

"Oh, okay. That's a relief."

The van came to a halt, and I could hear Bob's driver turn off the ignition. I squared my shoulders. "Let's do it, Bob."

"We are now facing Thirteenth Street. The parallel street is State. At first, we want to go to the northeast corner of 12th and State, to the Credit Union. Remember that place? The address is 1129 State. What direction do we need to go?"

How could I forget where I got stuck in the turnstile entrance? What did he ask me? The direction. I thought about reminding him of my poor sense of direction but didn't bother. I had one in four chances of getting it right. Pretty good odds. "North…uh, toward the lake, I guess."

"Yes, that's correct." He didn't sound surprised. But *I* was.

We made our way to our first destination. My cane technique seemed pretty good. Nice firm strokes back and forth across the sidewalk. We then headed downtown. At some point, I don't remember in which order, I crossed both State Street and Twelfth Street.

"You did that well. Just like a pro."

Yippee! I had crossed two major downtown streets on my own. My face turned into one huge grin. I felt like a jack-o-lantern with my heart a bright candle. If only everyone knew what I had accomplished! The adrenalin pumped into me.

"Okay, you said that you wanted to try eating at a restaurant. So I'm going to tell you the address, but it's up to you to locate it. I'm not sure myself where it is, so this will be a test for both of us."

What did he mean that he didn't even know where it was? Bob had designed this plan and the route himself. This was definitely the blind leading the blind.

We'd get through it. We always did.

As I made my way forward on the sidewalk, the space I had to maneuver seemed to shrink. What odd steel objects did my cane keep hitting?

"Explore them, Amy," Bob suggested when I asked him.

In order to "explore" them, I had to slide my cane up the sides of the obstacles as far as I could—knee- and waist-high in some cases—and reach out as far as necessary to make logical guesses. "They all seem to form different shapes. I can't identify them."

"They're flat lines and curves…." Bob sounded puzzled for a second then snapped his fingers. "That's right. Downtown Erie is having a block party this weekend," he recalled. "Let me check it out." I could hear the methodical tapping of his cane exploring the same types of obstacles I came up against.

"These must be tables and chairs set up on the sidewalk. That's what we are coming across. Yes, today we'll have to fight the crowds."

"Oh? Oh! A *block* party!" Lucky for me I had my sleep shades. Everyone would have seen the panic in my eyes. I held my cane close. How could I possibly make my way through the congested sidewalk? "Should we postpone our lesson for a more 'normal' day?"

"You're okay. People will move when they see you. If not, you'll find them with your cane. Just challenge yourself. Keep going."

We moved ahead in silence as I slowly battled my way through the maze of tables, chairs, and grills. I got in the habit of apologizing when I ran into people—or objects. "Oh, sorry!" I realized too late as I apologized to a pole.

The smells tantalized me.

I got a whiff of some kind of barbecue sauce…hickory? *Smells just like Dad's chicken used to, cooking on the grill.* Just a few feet ahead a sudden wave of heat hit me and I heard a crackle and sizzle. What was that? A couple of hot drops landed on my right arm. Grease. I jerked, speeded up and away from what I guessed was the vat of French fries cooking.

Next came the sweet onions wafting in my direction. And some kind of meat. Hamburgers? Steak? Must be burgers because…wasn't that dill pickles? Or, maybe…relish? So then, maybe hot dogs…my stomach growled.

The tip of my cane slapped against something metal. What in the world? A stroller? Oh my. I hope I didn't hit a baby with my cane. "Pardon me." I gulped and tapped away. Suddenly, I pitched forward. I felt a hand reach out to steady me. Before I could thank whoever helped me, he or she disappeared.

Now the smells had changed. I recognized coffee beans. Then I almost tripped over what felt like an electrical cord. I caught myself as I crashed into some sheet … metal. "Careful, lady," came the gruff voice. "Watch where you're going. There are a bunch of coffee pots—oh you can't see…."

As I moved forward again, I caught the tail end of an order. "…So I'll have a Bud." From the gushing that I heard, I guessed the beer was on tap. Some laughter followed, and an old, tinny voice cut through my thoughts. "Ye're a good fella. Keep it comin', son." I heard the loud smacking of wet lips and more laughter.

Suddenly, I couldn't move. I had boxed myself into a corner and got tangled up in the legs of whatever blocked the passage. I longed for a giant hand to lift me out and place me on the path again. *Where is the way through? A-m-y, focus! People must be staring.* "Uh…uh…Bob!"

"I'm here. You're doing great. Go ahead. I'm right behind you."

"No way, I'm stuck. There are like some cords and chairs and something big." The more trapped I felt, the squeakier my voice became. "Everywhere I turn, I'm just *stuck*. Why aren't they *helping* me? Why doesn't someone move something so I can get *out*?"

"I don't think anyone is there, or they would have." Bob's steady voice calmed me. I half-hoped that he would change places with me and take the lead. Obviously, I wasn't doing a good job on my own. Instead, he began to instruct me. "Can you reach out and touch the chair? You'll have to move it yourself if it's light. If not, turn around and inch yourself backward until you find space to move again."

Geez. He certainly doesn't mollycoddle me. He just believes I'll rise to the occasion.

Finding that I couldn't move the chair—which by now seemed wider and more like a table—I backed up, crossed over some kind of hose in the grass and timidly tapped the round ball of my cane around some bags and boxes before shifting forward. Once I could move, I could breathe freely again, and the claustrophobia receded. My breath came in quick, rasping pants. Maybe I was hyperventilating.

"Bob?" *pant! pant!* "Are you there? Bob. Where are we?" *pant!* "BOB!"

"I'm right beside you. Amy, are you all right?"

I trembled for a few seconds. "Yes, I'm fine."

"Good," he said matter-of-factly. "Now is the time to ask someone where we are."

Before I could get the words out of my mouth, I felt a sudden burst of air and a sweaty body brushed up against my arm as wheels whizzed by my now-vertical cane. What was that? A skateboard?

A female voice caught my attention. "Stop staring at them. That isn't nice." Someone laughed. Someone else mumbled. I strained to hear. *Did the woman mean Bob and me? Of course, everyone can see us. Just because we can't see them doesn't mean they can't see us. How quickly I forget.*

"Make way. Let 'em pass on by. Move yo' feet, boy."

"Yo' mama."

There would never be a good time to ask, but Bob was right, I needed to find out. "Uh…Excuse me? Could you tell me where we are?"

"Now you at Perry Square."

"Thank you."

"We have to cross one more street," Bob explained as if he'd known our location before I asked. "Lead the way, Sherlock."

I had almost finished crossing a side street when I heard a tough lady's voice "Hey, watch it. That's a six thousand dollar paint job on my bike!" I tilted my head toward the voice. She seemed to be shouting at … who? Me! "Yeah, that's right, chick-o, you!"

Me? I froze, terrified to take another step for fear my cane might do more damage. I was probably swinging it like a golf club without paying attention to where it landed. What if I had chipped her paint? This woman sounded seriously aggravated, as if she wanted to beat up this particular chick-o. What was I thinking? There must be a right and wrong way to arc my cane forward in a crowd, one that I hadn't yet learned. Bob, what about *that* lesson?

"Did I tell you that this is also the weekend for 'Roar on the Shore?'" Bob asked me dryly. "Eight thousand motorcyclists are gathered right here in the heart of downtown for the event."

I felt faint. "Well, I don't think I befriended *that* motorcycle mama."

"Come on, let's keep moving and find our target restaurant." Bob's voice took on a jovial tone meant to spur me forward. I took a long, deep breath and continued. "What address am I looking for?"

"I don't think the bistro is very far away, if I remember correct—" *Crunch!*

What just happened? It took only a second to figure it out. Oof! My cane had clashed with Bob's as if they were two swords coming to blows quite low near our shins. "Oh, sorry. I didn't know you had gone ahead."

"Quite all right to have a snag-up when two canes are in such close proximity." He didn't sound cross at all, thank goodness. "You're doing very, very well this afternoon," he added.

I glowed at his praise and vowed to listen better. Perfectly, if possible. I would align myself in all the right directions and prove him right. I cocked my head to listen to the voices around me. "Shall I ask what street we're on and the address here?"

"Go to it!"

A moment later when I heard a deep male voice, I found my opportunity. "Sir, could you please tell me the address here?"

"Not sure of the exact number but we're on Sassafras Street."

Bob clapped his hands together. "Bravo, Amy, exactly as I thought. We are not far from our destination." *How did he figure these things out?* "We need to get to number 2027. Are we on the correct street?"

Sassafras. "Yes," I affirmed.

"Will we stay on this side of the street or cross it? And then, which direction will we head?"

"We need to cross the street." Since it worked the first time, I guessed the same direction. "...an' uh, go north."

"We will cross Seventh from the northeast to the northwest corner," he corrected.

"Oh yeah, that's what I meant." I had no idea that we had even found our way to a corner.

"Good! I'm right behind you."

Maybe I could peek to make sure I was moving in the right direction. I had the important job of leading us across the street, after all. I could feel Bob's cane at my heels and speeded up. No chance to cheat now. I forced myself to listen for moving vehicles, and for the lull, which would indicate the traffic had stopped at a light. My adrenalin kicked in at the sudden silence. "Bob, we can cross." He listened for just a moment to verify it and said, "Correct."

Off we went. As usual, I wanted to race across. What if both of us had guessed wrong and the drivers of the cars didn't see us and started up again? But I forced myself to walk at an even pace until I felt the raised dots and the curb on the other side. *Whew! Made it!*

"Let's inquire as to this address," Bob suggested as we stepped over the curb. "There should be a building to the immediate left."

I slid my cane forward and eventually felt a smooth, wide stairway with shallow stone steps. "Here?"

"Go inside and find out."

I started climbing. *One. Two. Three. Four. Five. Okay. Top.* I felt for a door handle and pulled. We had entered a building. But was it the restaurant?

"Hullloohh!" I called and inquired as to the number of the building. "Yep, this is it, Bob. Let's eat!"

"My name is Dan, and I will be your server for the afternoon." The gentleman took my arm and escorted me to a round table on what I guessed to be the left-hand side of the room. He pulled out the chair, and I sat down. My stress drained away in this peaceful atmosphere. I folded my cane while Dan read the menu to us.

I could tell by the plush carpet beneath my feet, the silence surrounding us, and the impeccable manners of the waiter that Bob had chosen an upscale restaurant for our experiment. It suddenly dawned on me that was why our first stop was to the Credit Union.

"Madame?"

"Uh," I bit my lip. "I'll have a cup of wa—I mean espresso, " I amended. This place seemed far too elegant for my usual glass of water.

Bob didn't hesitate. "I'll have a black coffee."

After the waiter left, Bob spoke, "Tsk! Tsk! Much better for you to have found the seat on your own."

"Bob, have a heart. I deserved that break. We had a challenging afternoon. Imagine a Block Party and Roar on the Shore all in the same day. Isn't that amazing!"

"Why are you so amazed? You handled it well."

I laughed, warmed again by his praise. "Except for that big tangle-up in the one area."

When I heard the tinkling of liquid, I realized Dan had returned. I patted the table in front of me to find the glass. My hand came across something with a long thin stem. I tapped it. Then brought both hands to the object and walked my fingers up the stem. A wine glass for the water. I felt the cool condensation , on the outside rim.

Soon our coffees arrived. But as I reached for the miniature cup, I felt steam come off the rim and drew my hand back quickly. Better wait. I couldn't risk spilling it and burning myself.

"Madame? To eat?"

"Can you read the dessert menu?"

After listening to the choices, I decided on a thin crepe with two scoops of ice cream drenched in thick fudgy syrup, slathered in sticky caramel and topped with several slices of banana. If I had to wear these sleep shades, I might as well make eating as challenging as possible. I wasn't going to play it safe with a mere pudding I could just scoop onto a spoon. Bob settled on a piece of apple pie.

"This is my treat," I said, thrilled to make the offer. "It's the least I can do for all your help today."

"Very generous, indeed."

Bob explained that the best way to pinpoint utensils and food was to think of the space in front of me as the face of a round clock. "It will enable you to quickly locate each item and, hopefully, avoid spillage and dropping food onto your lap."

That knowledge could have helped me avoid knocking over several glasses of water and embarrassing myself in public over the past year or so.

A few minutes later, the waiter returned with our orders. "Madame." As if on cue, he described where my food was in the exact manner Bob had explained. "Your turtle crepe is directly in front of you at twelve o'clock. Your silverware is to the right of your plate. Your espresso is at two o'clock."

Dan really knew his stuff!

First, I delicately slid my fingertips around the rim of my plate. I didn't want my fancy dessert to slide onto the table and make a mess I couldn't clean up. Then I picked up my knife and fork and sliced the banana crepe. Although I wasn't sure this was proper to do, I poked my finger around my plate to ensure none of the pieces had moved near the edge.

Now I was ready to eat. I swished a slice of banana in the syrup and added a piece of crepe to the fork and slipped it into my mouth, dabbing it with the cloth napkin. It was not as easy as I thought. Intent on mastering my task, I didn't even talk to Bob until I had nearly finished my crepe. Finally, I carefully searched the table for the cup of espresso and took a sip.

"Bob, I'm so glad I could share my poem in Braille with you today," I began. "It starts out how I'm reaching for the sun, right? Then it describes this huge fall."

He was silent, so I continued explaining. "When I first wrote it, I intended it to mean how we all have doubts in our lives that cause us to fall from our plans. But when I was practicing my Braille, it took on a new, deeper meaning. It represented the actual fall at my high school reunion that ultimately caused me to seek help for my vision. Remember when I first met you, I didn't say much, and I avoided going for mobility training?"

"You did hesitate a little," he admitted. I heard his fork scrape against his dish.

"My poem described how the grass was like a green basinet and there, I rested and I was nursed with stillness. That was the silence when I didn't call you. God was speaking to my heart and trying to help me accept that I needed help with mobility. After I had 'nursed' enough I grew stronger and could stand on my own. That's when God prompted me to call you."

"Hmm. Amy, we all have our ways to cope. Yours is through your faith. Mine isn't."

I paused. "Bob, I know you must have felt so angry at God for taking your friend away. I wanted you to know that He heals us all in time if we let Him." I struggled for words to communicate the love I knew God had for Bob. "When we turn to Him, He shows us how to move forward."

Bob said, perhaps misunderstanding, "It's easy for some people to be optimistic. You're one of them. And you will succeed because you jump high on your 'perfumed dreams.'"

"Are you kidding me? I wouldn't even have had the courage to begin if it hadn't been for your persistence. You have taught me *so* much. But God has walked me through the entire process beyond even that. You know at the end of the poem, it says 'I long to touch the Son.' The word changed from sunshine to the son of God. That's what God is teaching me in my journey—to trust Him more this year." My voice grew earnest. "I just wanted to share that with you." *And also that I'm praying for you.*

"I appreciate your candor and I respect you." After a short silence, Bob said, "So what was the most challenging part of this afternoon's training session?"

As we chatted, I felt a little giddy from the enormity of the experience. Or maybe it was from the espresso. *Calm down, girl!*

"We'll have the check now," I informed Dan. "Can you read it to me?"

Once I learned the cost, I realized that I was faced with a new challenge. How was I going to know which bills to use? I unzipped the pack around my waist and extracted both bills. *Which was the ten and which was the one?* I asked the waiter to identify each one for me and later, to count back my change.

After the waiter left, Bob cleared his throat. "Now if you want to be certain about your money and to keep your independence, pay close attention to what I am going to say next."

Bob launched into an explanation of the different ways to fold various money denominations to distinguish them from each other. "So if you want to find a five-dollar bill, fold it in half the short way. And if you have a twenty-dollar bill, fold it in half lengthwise," Bob concluded.

"I never even thought of that before," I exclaimed, wondering where my good friend, Dan, was. I expected him to escort me to the front door of the restaurant, but no such luck. He had disappeared. Nevertheless, I led the way out of the restaurant without difficulty, fumbling only when I tried to locate the main door. Otherwise, I held my head high with my confidence soaring even higher.

"Bob, what was the name of that waitress who helped me find the door?" I asked afterward.

"Waitress? No, she wasn't a waitress. That woman was standing right outside the door. My guess—she was just attending the block party and made herself useful."

"Oh. I thought for sure she worked at the restaurant."

Bob continued to awe me by knowing such things. But the very best thing about my day at that moment was the van located just across the street. Finally, I could take my sleep shades off.

Thank You, thank You, thank You, God, for getting me through this afternoon!

I joked and laughed with Bob and his driver all the way home. "Roger, you wouldn't believe this Motorcycle Mama who yelled at me. I was terrified to move. I thought she would hit me!"

"How can anyone be that mean to our Amy?" Roger asked.

Though I laughed, I remembered Bob's reaction during our training. He didn't excuse her. Rather he explained with a hint of humor in his voice why I found myself facing her. Our paths crossed only because we were both downtown at the same time.

My trainer had learned to sweep away negative criticism as easily as he took the next sweep of his cane to move forward. The more I thought about it, the more I liked his approach. Bob always taught me more than good mobility techniques. He also modeled an attitude that would bring me success.

That's when I remembered my attitude at the start of the day's journey when I felt Satan was trying to rob me of my confidence. I wondered if God had sent me to Erie in the middle of the block party and motorcycle extravaganza to purposely demonstrate that Bob and I could accomplish abundantly more than I had ever dreamed possible.

It sure seemed right to me.

Chapter 23
PURSUING IN-DEPTH TRAINING

"Have you heard anything about more training?" Mindy asked as she settled in her chair and bit into her eggroll.

"Nope." I motioned to the waitress to bring me a set of disposable chopsticks. "My caseworker, Rita, is totally overworked so I guess she hasn't found time to answer."

With an apologetic smile, the Chinese waitress handed me the chopsticks, using both hands to be polite. I was a "regular," and she knew I preferred them to silverware. I slid the paper off and broke them in two, then lifted a piece of sweet and sour chicken to my lips.

"You need to follow up on the training. We're more than halfway through summer."

"I know. I already called Rita. She said I have a couple of possibilities. There's the center in Pittsburgh, another in Cleveland, and, of course, the one in Louisiana. That one's a long-term program, almost a year."

"Okay, I just don't want you to miss out on the opportunity. You know how you put things off, especially if it's not something you're crazy about."

I rolled my eyes at my high school friend. "I promise you," I declared, my hand on my heart, "I'm not procrastinating. I want to do this training." In fact, I felt antsy waiting to hear about it.

But Mindy was right. I had been in denial and had put off seeking help for years. She had kept after me. I thought about the past year and how difficult it had been for me to accept, one step at a time, that I was losing my sight. I didn't like Bob at first. I didn't appreciate my cane. I hated other people seeing it and making wide detours away from me, as if I had a disease. But little by little, I realized, as much as I disliked it, if I wanted to have a healthy and productive future, I needed to accept my situation and to do something about it. I had to choose to move forward.

I missed my old life. How wonderful it would be to pick up where I left off, to go back overseas where I could teach and travel as much as I wanted! I hadn't traveled anywhere, even in the United States, for nearly four years. But none of us can turn back time, so in that way, I was like everyone else. I had to adjust.

And to be grateful.

Mindy rounded up a stray piece of broccoli in a light sauce and speared it with her fork along with a piece of beef. "Do you have any preference as to where you'd like to get your training?"

"Yeah! It would be great to fly to Louisiana and get into that program. You know, the students there have to rappel down walls, build some project with electric tools, and find their way around campus blindfolded in a timed exercise," I said.

The mere thought of it excited me. I knew I was still holding onto remnants of my old lifestyle. The "adventure" part of me longed to participate. It was like going to Africa on safari or learning Arabic in Yemen. I wanted to say I had done it, probably more than I wanted to actually do it.

Mindy took a sip of her Diet Coke. "Didn't you just say that was a longer program?"

I groaned. "Yeah, I probably won't be able to go there if I plan to keep my teaching job. I called the director, and she said they could make allowances for shorter periods, but I'd probably have to go for at least three months. Too bad," I said, clearing my plate of the fried rice and shrimp.

"If you keep your teaching job? You mean you might be willing to give up your job?" Mindy looked surprised. The waitress came by and set our bill on the table. My friend handed me a cookie and took out her wallet. This was her day to treat.

"No, no. Mindy, you know how difficult it was for me to get this teaching job. I couldn't just give it up." That's what the logical side of me said.

But the adventure-seeking side screamed for me to take on the Louisiana training. Why not? Just go to Ruston. I'd never been there. Experience culture in the South. Like Bob said, I could even take classes at Louisiana Tech in conjunction with the Blind Center. I'd never find this opportunity again. Do it! Go!

"Glad to hear that." Mindy interrupted my thoughts. "Your family needs you at home, especially your mom." She broke the cookie apart and read, 'Happy news is on its way to you.'"

I broke open mine, tossed a crunchy fragment into my mouth and swallowed before I read the scrap of paper. "'Good luck is the result of good planning.' As usual, our fortunes are reversed. Happy news is probably on its way to *me*. I'm definitely not the planner. You are."

"There you go," she said with a laugh, handing me the small typed fortune. "This means you'll hear back from your caseworker soon. And I'm going to claim good luck from my careful planning." She reached for the fortune I held out. We had a running joke that we always picked up the wrong cookie and received each other's fortune by mistake.

That night, I became impatient. What if I never heard back from Rita? I needed to receive training this summer while I was on the caseload of the Bureau of Blindness. I had only one more session with Bob, and then I'd be out on the streets, so to speak—in more ways than one. If I wanted the training, I'd have to push. Otherwise, it would pass me by. When Bob and I finished our mobility training, the BBVS would have done all they could for me, and I would have to sign off on the paperwork. Their role was to ensure that I received enough training and assistance to secure a job, which I had.

They had provided me with hearing aids, a cane, a laptop computer and a nineteen-inch flat screen for my existing computer as well as a closed circuit TV, which enabled me to magnify anything printed. I'd received a parking placard that allowed me to use handicapped parking spots. Plus, I had access to talking and large-print books from the Carnegie Library of the Blind, and other paraphernalia, including bright lights, to make my life easier. That didn't even include the hearing and vision exams, the counseling, and Bob's training. All this cost the state a bundle. Did I have a right to ask for more?

According to Bob, I did.

I have to be proactive. I sat down at my computer and wrote Rita a long email asking her to liaise with me for the training as soon as possible. I emphasized how imperative it was that I received it now. As I finished, my cell phone rang. I glanced at the name: Julio, my friend.

"Listen to this, Julio." I read him the email I had just drafted.

"What? Slow down and read it to me again." Impatiently, I did. But I could tell he hadn't understood. "Do you need me to send it to you?"

"Yes, you're reading it way too fast, and I can't hear you very well."

"What? Are you back at Starbucks? Okay." I forwarded my email to him and hung up, waiting for him to call back.

He returned the call in less than a minute.

"Do not send that email," he advised. "That's crazy."

"What? Why? What are you talking about?" I lowered my head onto the table. It was nearly midnight. I didn't even want to think about starting all over again.

"You can't send that, Miss I'm-only-defending-my-human-rights Bovaird."

"What?"

I can't remember exactly how I worded my email, but Julio insisted that night I was demanding more training because I was entitled to it, as if Rita was purposely and unfeelingly withholding my basic human rights.

"Come on!" I exploded. "I have no idea what you mean."

"Well, all I'm saying is if you send that email, I can guarantee you will hear back from Rita. But it won't be what you expect. Sheesh."

I wondered what part sounded demanding. Thank God, I'd read it to Julio before sending it out. I would never want to come across as ungrateful or pushy. But I didn't want Rita to get caught up in all her other clients, and forget about what she had promised me. Time was critical. It was nearly August and summer would be over before my training was even approved.

That night, Julio and I redrafted an email that he deemed appropriate for me to send. It took nearly two hours, but since Julio lived on the west coast, the time factor didn't affect him at all. He had so much patience with me.

"Thanks, Julio. Now I can go ahead and send it, right?"

"Yes, why not?" He sounded annoyed. "This is much better. You come across as professional. Your counselor can see how the intensive training will actually *save* the government money by keeping you employed. That's what you want her to see, right?"

"Of course." I yawned. "Okay, I'm ready to hit SEND, so … nothing else I need to add?"

"No. Send it already."

A few days later I received my response from Rita, and shared it with Mom. "All systems 'GO!' I just need to know where I'm going."

Later that day, I received a phone call from my sister. "So I hear you're all set for more in-depth training. That's great news." She and her husband offered to drive me to the Cleveland Sight Center to check it out. "It's close, so we can bring Mom on the weekends. We can even take you home if you want to come," she said.

Did I? It was a far cry from the independent training I envisioned in Louisiana, but it would probably suit our family situation better. I would have to wait and see what our visit brought.

"If you'd like, we can take you this Friday," Carolyn said. "I have to work second shift at the prison, but if we get an early start, we'll be back in time."

"That would be great!" I was touched that they offered to take time out of their busy schedules, so I could get a glimpse of what the training program offered in Cleveland. "I need to call the director to see if that works with them."

"Let us know as soon as you find out."

That morning, the skies looked dark and overcast, but the rain held off for awhile. We planned for only a couple hours of driving, and that included time set aside for finding the center. The director, a laid-back but direct woman in charge of the Adjustment to Blindness Program, had given me explicit directions over the phone. We had no problem finding the building or parking.

A security guard pointed out the correct floor.

My brother-in-law, Dave, held out his hand. "Thank you."

The building's long corridors looked clean and well-kept. The floors gleamed. We found our way to Suzanne's office and stepped through the door.

At first we didn't see anyone, so we seated ourselves in the waiting area. Suzanne arrived shortly with her guide dog. She removed her rain jacket and shook the water off her curly blondish-brown hair; the rain had finally started. After removing the harness from her yellow Lab, she exclaimed, "The sky opened up on us!" With that, she smiled and extended her hand, making the three of us feel welcome.

Suzanne was blind. I didn't know if that meant a hundred percent or if she had some residual vision, and in time, I asked her. She explained that she had lost much of her vision through the same disease I had. Wow! I thought it interesting that I reacted so differently to her than I had to Bob. He had done a good job of preparing me to meet other vision-impaired people.

We sat at a round table as she "interviewed" me to find out what I was looking for. "You're in luck," she said with a hearty laugh. "We just finished up a six-week program with a large group of sixteen to twenty-two year olds this week." She waved the air and said, "Boy, were we ever busy. That translates to 'They exhausted us.'" She laughed again. "But they always get a lot out of it, so it's worth it. They stay in our residential apartments," she added.

"What kind of training do they receive?" I asked, rubbing my bare arms to warm them in the air conditioning.

"Independent living, survival skills, orientation and mobility, technology, financial aid, and scholarship counseling, career guidance, recreational and social skills, is the gist of it." Suzanne ticked them off on her fingers.

"Hmm." I wondered how they coped with having so many canes in such close proximity.

She was intent on selling the program to me. "If you can come, say, in a week or so, we can further evaluate your needs and set up an effective, personalized plan catered to you. By that, I mean we can easily tailor the program."

"That's wonderful. I need more mobility training, some life skills, like cooking and that kind of thing." I thought for a moment. "Definitely more

Braille. I'd like a lot of Braille. And I'd like to do it all ... um, under sleep shades."

"For eight hours?" She put her hands on her hips and whistled. "You *are* serious about learning. Always a good sign. We can certainly accommodate that. If you start to feel tired or drained, you can always take them off."

"Oh, no. I'll be fine."

She stood up. The yellow Lab came out from under the table, stretched his front paws and stood beside Suzanne. "Would you like a tour of the facilities?"

Dave, who up until this point had been silent in order to allow me to state my business, spoke up, "That would be super. We'd love to see what you have."

Suzanne called her assistant, Tonya, into the office and introduced us. She looked a little younger, but had the same welcoming smile. They joked easily with each other and talked back and forth about finding the keys, but finally Tonya decided that she had the ones she needed for our tour. We would meet Suzanne back in the office shortly.

Tonya used a cane and explained that her near-blindness was caused by Retinitis Pigmentosa, too. "I apologize in advance because sometimes I have mishaps." She laughed warmly. "Don't be surprised if that happens along the way."

"We're used to that with Amy," Carolyn said, with a smile to lighten the words.

Tonya stopped in front of a closed door and explained that someone read the news out loud each morning from that room. We walked to a second door. "This is where we conduct job training," she explained. "Some people learn how to be telephone operators. Others learn different job-related tasks."

"That's great!" I said, thinking there was hope for me if I took the training in Louisiana and lost my job.

We walked down another hallway. "This is the pre-school area for early intervention." As she took us to the different departments, she spoke in acronyms and abbreviations just like I had when I worked for the military in San Antonio. All jobs seemed to have that kind of system.

We entered an elevator, and went to the third floor. When we exited, we took a short walk and turned left, stopping abruptly in front of the second door. "Now where is that keyhole?" Tonya mumbled, more to herself than to us. "I want to show you the apartments available for our temporary residents." At last the door swung open, and we walked in. The apartment included a kitchenette, a small living room with a television and a lounge chair, a bedroom and a bath.

Carolyn peered into the kitchen and opened the fridge to peek inside. "Nice, Amy. Convenient. You can practice in this kitchen what you learn in your training." She looked around the apartment. "These rooms look comfortable."

"Yeah, I can see." I said, impressed. I immediately covered my mouth with both hands, my face red. I hoped Tonya didn't think I meant that I could and she couldn't, as in, "Bully for me." Leave it to me to hurt someone's feelings. When she didn't take any notice of my blunder, I relaxed.

Tonya continued her explanation. "Whenever possible, we rent our rooms to family members of those receiving treatment at the Cleveland Clinic," she said referring to one of the top-ranking hospitals in the US. Her voice lowered to a hush. "Our price is quite reasonable. We do this as a service."

Dave asked, "How far away is the Cleveland Clinic?" He crossed his arms as he listened for her response. He seemed so serious. But then, the Cleveland Clinic was a hospital for serious diseases.

She swept her cane in jerky movements as she located the door. "Just a few blocks."

I thought, *It's not like I'm going to the Cleveland Clinic or anything. Blindness is not life-threatening.* It felt odd to be so close to a hospital that treated life and death illnesses. But the Sight Center seemed to have a heart for people, so why not rent the rooms to aid family members of those facing such odds?

We filed out of the apartment. After pulling the door closed and locking it, Tonya led us to the elevator and pressed the button to another floor. "We even have a bowling alley," she said proudly, gesturing to the basement level. "Would you like to see it?"

Dave spoke for all of us. "Sure!"

I hadn't been bowling in decades, but it seemed to be an asset to the sight program. I recalled how Dorothy Stiefel, founder of TARP (Texas Association of Retinitis Pigmentosa) and the author of the first books I read about RP and Usher's Syndrome, had said she excelled at bowling. She maintained that her restricted tunnel vision could block out any distraction and she could focus solely on the pins. "Ah, there must be truth in that," I whispered to myself. "No wonder they have a bowling alley." More loudly, I said to Tonya, "I'll bet the teenagers love it."

"They do," she assured me.

We made our way back to the main office and said our goodbyes to both women. "I'll let you know soon," I promised.

"The sooner, the better," Suzanne warned. "Our caseload can change quickly."

As soon as we left, I asked my family what they thought.

"They impressed me," Dave said immediately.

"Amy, we have to cross the road here," my sister cautioned. After we crossed, she went on, "They were knowledgeable, kind, and warm-hearted. Didn't at least one of the women have what you have?"

"RP? Yes, I think they both did."

My sister's voice took on a reverential tone. "And it's *tailored* to you. I don't know how many places would do that. If it were me, I'd come here in a heartbeat. But you have to make up your own mind."

"I think this might be God's answer to my prayer," I said slowly. I had really wanted to go to Louisiana, but maybe for the wrong motives.

Louisiana pointed to adventure and excitement.

The center in Cleveland provided excellent training with the added benefit of reassuring my family that I would be nearby if they needed me. God seemed to be saying, "Now I want you to put away childish ideas and put on the cloak of responsibility."

That afternoon I felt an indelible "rightness" about receiving my training in Cleveland. It had to be God's will for me. How good God was to reveal His heart and bring my more shallow plans to light!

How grateful I was that God was maturing me.

Chapter 24
The Dreaded Drop Route

Everything I knew about drop routes came from a Walt Disney movie about an attempt to lower a full-grown elephant from a cargo plane into a remote village. The military's planned drop went awry while the *unplanned* journey brought on the laughs.

When Bob explained that our last mobility lesson involved a planned drop route, sweat drops of my own fell. Deposited who-knows-where, I faced the menacing task of finding Bob's office in a thick jungle of city streets.

My eyes slid back to Bob's email. I reread the details, trying not to let his "pointers" intimidate me. Heavily peppered with cardinal directions—that alone made my heart race—it delineated my boundaries, none of which were familiar to me since the only time I *ever* explored the city center was with Bob. Did he think he was dealing with Superwoman?

The goal was to use my environmental cues to help me find my way to Bob's office. Listed, they seemed do-able. I would simply have to pay attention to the traffic flow, note the position of the sun, and pick up on familiar non-visual landmarks. The problem I had never shared with Bob was that I truly *was* directionally-challenged. In short, I had a history of getting lost.

I don't know how I traveled around the world by myself. My family often whipped out the story, "Remember when you got lost finding your way home from Bible school in our hometown?"

The fact that I was only four or five years old didn't matter. When I left the church, I didn't find anyone waiting to take me home. I thought they had forgotten me. So I set out on my own. But nothing looked familiar. I saw lots of houses and enormous, leafy trees. My steps grew slower and more timid. So many ferocious trees. I tried to ignore them; they spooked me. I imagined monsters lurked in each one. When I passed, I knew they planned to grab me…any second. That's why no one else played outside—because of the tree monsters. *Was I the last little girl alive?*

The scary trees gave way to a field, and then I had to cross a railroad track. A long brick building leered at me. I turned and ran back over the tracks. There, I saw another long and narrow building. Then I found a door. Panting, I tapped on the door, barely making a sound. But someone heard. The lady who answered looked familiar, and she smelled nice. I took a deep breath and wanted to explain that I was lost but couldn't find the courage to admit it. Of course, living in a small town, she knew my mother—in fact, she had lived right next door to my family for three years so she called my mother and told her where to pick me up. Though it seemed I had walked for hours and covered miles, I was still on the same street as the church.

As I scrolled through Bob's email, I felt like that lost child all over again.

He naively thought I had enough skills to identify a street I knew and navigate my way to the right address, just by listening to the flow of traffic. The street boundaries listed might help others, but not me. I couldn't form a mental picture of them. If that method didn't work, perhaps Bob's back-up plan included the train. The whistle and the sound of the wheels moving on the track might indicate its direction. Just my luck I would be standing *on* the tracks when I tried to orient myself with the sound. I shuddered. Of course, if both these methods failed me, I had the position of the sun to guide me. But what if the sun didn't shine? And what did Bob mean exactly by "familiar non-visual landmarks?"

I wanted to throw up.

Every time I thought about the email, I felt queasy. When Julio called, I shared my fears.

He replied, "It's a test, a *cumulative* test of your skills, what did you expect?"

"Well, at least the elephant in *Operation Dumbo Drop* had two Green Berets to guide him to the remote village."

"As usual, I have no idea what you're referring to," Julio said. "But I can guarantee that Dumbo didn't receive training like you did and, therefore, did not require a test."

"How can I be tested on something I've never learned before? This will be the first time I've tried these methods."

"Whatever. He's *exposing* you to them. Get over it."

I thought for a minute. "Well, Bob did say I could 'gather information' three times during the session, but only forty-five minutes apart. He called them my 'get-out-of-jail' cards," I said, suddenly recalling the term.

Julio laughed. "I like Bob. He has a good sense of humor."

I sweltered in the July heat. Without air conditioning, my blinds hung limp, and I couldn't concentrate. "Hang on, Julio." While I adjusted the wooden slats over the windows, I felt a sharp twinge of pain. "Hey!" I slapped at my arm just above the elbow. "A mosquito just bit me." I leaned in and noticed the screen was cracked open. "No wonder," I muttered.

"Forget the mosquitoes. What were you saying?

"You didn't read that email. He's a *control* freak. Well, maybe not that bad. He gave me two hours and fifteen minutes to find my way."

"That's a long time. You can do it."

I wasn't that five year old anymore. I would have to keep a positive mindset and use those methods Bob wanted me to use. If I had known how to use the flow of traffic, especially the *train* traffic to guide me when I was lost, then maybe I could have found my way home from Bible school.

On the appointed day, I had my sleep shades on, as instructed, before I entered the van. "Let's head … head out," I said, pretending to sob.

"Did you receive my email?" Bob asked, ignoring my melodramatics. I could hear the excitement in his voice.

I made a face. Of course, Bob couldn't see it. "Yeah, I got it."

"Unlike the last time, I wanted to give you a head's up, so you'd know what to expect. It's going to be challenging for us. I told my driver not to tell even me where he plans to drop us off."

My jaw dropped. Although Bob spoke in his "serious" voice, I could tell that he enjoyed this part of his job. What seemed like "controlling," he had meant as carefully planned guidelines to challenge both of us. While he knew the parameters and the means to locate his office, he would also be tested by the variables. Although not a game, it certainly made for a stimulating activity that Bob relished. This must be how he kept himself sharp. Seen from this angle, it didn't seem quite so overwhelming, though I still lacked the essential skills to find my way.

I remembered to ask Bob what he meant by non-visual landmarks.

He threw the question back at me. "If you can't see them, how will you know they're familiar landmarks?"

"I know—*exactly*!" When he didn't elaborate, I realized he was waiting for me to figure it out. "By the smell? Or maybe how they feel?" I imagined groping one of the oversized carved fish statues placed around the city "Can

I recognize a landmark by how it sounds?"

"You've got the right idea."

I rubbed my hands together in anticipation. "So if I smell chocolate, chances are we're at *Stefanelli's* or at least nearby, is that right?"

"Quite right, however, we will not be in that vicinity today."

"Oh, just my luck," I slumped back in the seat. "My *bad* luck."

Bob chuckled. "No matter. Our route will not disappoint you. I can guarantee that. Are you prepared?"

"As ready as I'll ever be," I said, biting my thumbnail. I planned to choose a direction and stick with that for awhile. I would ask my first question soon enough and eventually use all my 'Get out of jail' cards.

The van stopped a few minutes later. *Just get it over with.* I hopped out, finding the curb with my cane. I stood next to the van and waited for Bob to provide any last-minute instructions.

"What's the first thing you need to do?" Bob asked.

"I guess see which … direction the traffic … is going?"

"Are you sure?"

Was I? "I think so."

"Yes, that's correct. However, when you're in a situation like this, you need to set your plan and follow it. Don't doubt yourself. That's when you get into trouble, especially if you're not sure if you should cross the street or not. You cannot hesitate. If you're not careful, indecision can cost you time, effort, and even your life."

"Okay." I took a deep breath. "By the way, I'd never think twice when crossing a street. I'd make a dash for it! You should know that!" I grinned. We had discussed this many times. "The traffic is going right so that's … north." I hoped it was. "I think we need to go east." His office was on East Thirteenth Street so that seemed logical.

I didn't know how to link the direction of the traffic flow to the direction I needed to travel to reach my destination, nor did I know if I was permitted to ask.

Bob didn't give me any inkling whether I had chosen correctly or not. He simply let me lead.

We moved in silence for some time until I said, "Hey, where's the sun?" I put an arm out to feel the warmth of the sunlight. "Isn't its direction supposed to be one of our clues?" We all know that the sun rises in the east and sets in the west, but where was the sun at two o'clock? I tilted my face toward the sky but couldn't feel any warmth; it must have been cloudy.

Great job there, sunshine! A smattering of lyrics—from where, I had no idea—whipped around in my brain. *Oh Mr. Sun, Sun, Mr. Golden Sun, could you please shine down on me?* Even asking politely, it refused to assist.

If I had the benefit of the sun, I wasn't sure how that information would help me find my way to Bob's office.

As we continued our exploration, neither of us spoke. Finally, Bob broke the silence. "Do you notice any landmarks yet? Tap your cane to the right. Shoreline it." Bob was telling me to find out if there was a constant barrier to the right, and if so, what was it?

"I don't know, Bob, it seems as if we've been walking along this high barrier for quite awhile. Do you think it's a wall?"

"Feel it with your cane," he suggested. "Is that what it feels like?"

I tapped lightly, first low and worked my cane higher. "No-o, not a wall, something else … I'm not sure what."

We kept going. "This barrier has regular holes in it, Bob. It's narrow and the holes are, too. The space is straight up and down. Ooh." I bit my lip, concentrating. I felt intrigued as if I were trying to figure out the contents of a wrapped birthday gift. "What could it be?"

"Hmm." Bob knew, I could tell. "Stop and feel it with your hand. What's the texture?" By the clues he was feeding me, it was as if he was bursting for me to open the present.

"Well, it's thin and heavy and well-defined." A sudden guess came to me. "Bob! Is it a cemetery gate?" I had to know.

"I think it…is!" I detected unmistakable triumph in his voice. He continued. "So, what does *this* mean?"

I groaned but had no idea. I'd better come up with something so I didn't let him down. *Where are the cemeteries in Erie? Could we be passing by the McDonald's on Peninsula Drive?* I had a dim recollection of driving past a cemetery there with my dad. Was this street one of the parameters included in the email? *Think.*

Bob pushed me."Which direction do we need to go?"

I shrugged and bit my bottom lip. "Let's keep going this way." We probably needed to turn, but which direction? I doggedly led us in the same direction until I remembered my 'Get-out-of-jail' key. "Let's ask someone."

Just then, the sun came out directly overhead. I was still trying to figure out how the sun would help me when I heard Bob shout, "Amy, stop!" The urgency caused my heart to race. Mid-step, I stood on one foot, trembling. *Did I do something wrong? Could I get hit? Did I endanger the life of my trainer?*

"Do you hear that sound in front of you?" This time Bob spoke in a calm voice.

I put my foot down and listened with my whole body, my heart still pumping loudly in my chest. I heard a humming sound. I focused. A light rumbling. A motor of some sort. "Hmm, it's a vehicle. But it must not be moving…now. *I must have been right in its path a moment ago.*

Why wasn't it moving? Where was it? "It's…right in front of me, I think. Yes, it is, Bob. Oh. That's where you said it was."

Neither of us made a move. I finally realized Bob was waiting for me to get my bearings. "Oh-h, I get it. Okay, I'll ask."

Instead of walking around the vehicle to let it pass and ask someone on the street, I found the driver's window and tapped directly on it.

A muffled—and startled—woman's voice sounded behind the glass. "Oh my! What?! May I…may I…help you?" She sounded almost…*afraid.* I realized then that maybe I'd been a little too direct. When you can't see, you lose a sense of propriety. I wondered how Bob and I appeared to her— with our dual long canes and me, with my sleep shades. Did the canes seem like weapons? Did we look scary or intimidating … like robbers?

Bob softened my disruption. "Maybe this kind woman will help us out." He waited for me to pick up the reins and ask my question.

"Excuse me. Sorry to scare you. Can you please tell me what street we're on and uh, which direction we're heading?"

She gave us some street named after a tree, which clued Bob in on our whereabouts. "A-ha!" he exclaimed. I still had no idea where we were but at least I knew we were headed in the correct direction. That's when I started making progress. I picked up on Bob's excitement and keyed in on his cues. At first, his voice gave it away.

"Bob, I think we need to turn this corner, don't we?"

"Why do you think that?" He sounded like he was right next to me.

"It has to be close since the named streets go east and west, right?"

"East and west?"

His voice told me I had it backwards. "I meant north and south," I amended, "and your office is on East Thirteenth, so…we have to change directions."

"Good call," he approved.

I laughed, pleased with myself, and began to make more informed choices or at least better guesses. The specifics of our lesson interested me, and I was more willing to take risks with my decisions.

"There are stairs here, Bob." I tried to steer away from them to avoid falling sideways down them.

"Wait a minute. Stairs? Back up. Let's follow them and see where they go," Bob suggested.

"Okay." I tapped my cane to the edge of each step before moving to the next one, my arm extended each time. "There are a lot of steps!" I came to a stop as I realized we were below street level. Suddenly, several helpful clues came to me. First, I noticed it was darker than usual, which was weird since wearing sleep shades makes everything dark already. But if the sun were out, I could sense it through the degree of darkness. It was really dark now. An earthy, concrete rather musty smell permeated the still air. "Bob..." My voice echoed

"Did you have a question?" *Have a Question.* Another echo.

We *had* to be inside. Were we in some kind of tunnel? What would a tunnel have? Trains! "Bob, are we at a *railroad* crossing or underground train station?"

Bob's voice lowered, full of frustration. "Oh, darn. No train so no help here." I heard a sigh, and smiled. I knew the feeling Bob was experiencing: the teacher's plan fell through. He was counting on the train in our lesson. I wanted to giggle because my own teacher's plans have gone astray many times in my teaching career. Bob continued, "Very important clue, Amy. If you hear a train coming...."

I interrupted him. "Make sure I'm not standing on the tracks!"

I meant to be funny, but Bob was all business, ignoring my attempt at humor. "Not only should you pay attention if you do hear a train, listen for the direction in which it moves and the speed."

"Oh, I'll definitely listen for the speed, all right, and make sure I'm out of the way!"

"Disappointing to say the least," he mumbled. "It's a great tool to aid in orienting oneself."

We climbed the steps to the street level and continued on our way. It wasn't long until we arrived at our destination, a mere fifteen minutes late. My early aimlessness slowed us down, I presumed.

When we arrived at Bob's office building, I jumped up and down. "We made it! We *made* it." I didn't know if I had found the way to the office through my own skills, or if Bob's verbal clues had played the larger hand. Had I trusted them more than the true physical landmarks? Maybe I succeeded because of both. By navigating my way in sleep shades—in complete darkness—I felt as if I were one hundred percent blind. Yet I could make it.

Bob turned to me. "Let's get the elevator. We need to go to the third floor."

The third floor? Déjà vu. "Of course." I lifted my right hand and felt for the Braille I knew would be next to the elevator floor button. I ran my fingers over the dots slowly. "Here it is."

"Excellent. Now, press the button." He started whistling.

His high spirits matched mine, and all at once, an idea came to me. "Bob, can we see if Rita's in the office today?" I couldn't wait to share my newest accomplishment with my caseworker. She acted like my biggest fan and always had encouraging words.

"Let me see if I can find her."

I knew Bob would scour the building in an attempt to please me. I heard him leave and beamed, leaning on my cane. In a few minutes, I was rewarded with the sound of their voices. "Rita, is that you?"

"Yes, it's me. I'm hearing wonderful news about you today."

I turned toward her voice, twirling in a circle before I located it. I had forgotten to remove my sleep shades. "I'm over here. I did it! Bob and I had an awesome drop route lesson. He didn't even know where we were when we got dropped off. He wanted to challenge himself, too. Can you imagine?" The adrenalin of success made me bubble over. "But we made it, no thanks to the trains!"

Bob explained, still disappointed, "She means, one of the best methods of orienting oneself is by the direction and speed of moving trains. We didn't find one today."

"Now I understand. But you still made it here despite the lack of train traffic," Rita said. "Awesome. Even better."

"You know, I was dreading this lesson. But after we started, Bob made it seem like the most exciting adventure ever, and I couldn't give up. He forced me to use all my skills, especially my hearing." *Yes, in spite of my hearing loss, I'd tuned in better than ever.* I had to stop and catch my breath, but I never stopped smiling. "Bob is the best!"

"No, you did this on your own," he said firmly. "I just guided you ... and perhaps, gave you a few tools."

"Guided me to accomplish my best work," I said, laughing. "Bob, don't forget I'm a teacher, too. Once you motivate someone, you've *got* them. Did you mention tools? Yes, that's right. Remember when you told me that if I lost my sight before you gave me the tools to cope, you'd blame yourself?" I grinned all over. "Well, I now have a tool belt on which to hang them."

I felt like I could jump up and do a handstand right there in the hallway.

"You're doing so great!" Rita patted my shoulder. "I'm not sure I could do what you guys did today." Rita was sighted, but she went through various training programs wearing sleep shades to understand how her clients felt.

"It's not me," I admitted. "Bob pushes me to do these things. He expects it from me. How could I let him down? Rita, you are my witness." I turned toward where I thought Bob was standing. "Bob, you have changed my entire outlook toward my future. You made me want to excel in every aspect of training, even with Braille, and that doesn't have anything to do with mobility." I grinned and chattered about the experience, still completely wowed. Then I turned... and walked directly into the wall.

I felt Rita's hands as she reached out to aid me. "Oh Amy, are you okay?"

"S-sure." *Ow!* That had hurt! Not only my head, but also my pride, and it smacked some sense into me. I remembered I still had so much to learn. Thank God, I would receive two or three weeks of intensive training in Cleveland.

Rita still sounded concerned. "There's a lump forming on your forehead. Should I bring some ice?"

If she only knew how many lumps, bumps, and bruises my head had collected. Builders wear hard hats. This builder wore a hard *head*. In spite of my success, I knew I would face days of discouragement with my eyesight. I would walk into more walls, receive more bumps, bruises, cuts, and scrapes. But I would get through them with my tools. In addition to what I had learned in mobility training, I had developed a good sense of humor and still possessed a strong dose of optimism. "No. I'll be just fine."

God gives us these ultra-amazing days along the way to carry us past the others. I laughed and tapped the floor with the tip of my cane "This magic wand and I will take on my future—whatever that holds," I told Bob and Rita.

What a fabulous, momentous final day of training!

"I don't know downtown Erie well, but I'm going to practice until I learn it. I'll visit more cultural sites and attend more functions. I'll learn my way around." There was a lifetime of exploring to look forward to. "If I can master Erie, I can master San Antonio—I used to live there—and even San Diego… then São Paulo. I can even climb Machu Picchu, my longtime dream."

"You dream high, don't you?" Rita was chuckling.

"What type of a place is Machu Picchu and where is it located?" Bob asked.

"Machu Picchu is in Peru. I'm talking about the famous ruins of an Inca civilization high in the Andes Mountains. It's one of the seven world wonders," I informed him. "At eight thousand feet, it will be a challenge to reach, but I'll prepare myself."

"I'm sure you will," Bob said after giving it some thought. "I wish you luck."

"Well, I speak Spanish, and I love high mountains. I *will* go one day, so when you receive a postcard with a Peruvian stamp, you'll know it's from me." I could see myself, climbing rocky boulders and wearing a rain poncho in the highest altitudes. "And I can teach overseas again."

My mind swam with the possibilities.

"You'll do great!" Bob crowed. "By the way, you passed the test today with flying colors."

"Thank you." I reached out my hand and tapped Bob on the wrist. "Will I receive a certificate?"

"Does it matter?" Bob asked, suddenly serious.

I thought for a minute and shook my head. "*Mobility* matters. Mobility *matters*!" It was a revelation. "It allows me to join the rest of society, to follow my interests and passions, and mobility reconnects me with my love for traveling. I don't have to stay at home fearing the dark anymore. I can live independently."

Suddenly I realized that God had answered questions that had burdened me for over twenty-five years. *When I lost my vision, could I still teach? Or would I be a burden to my family? Would I even be able to leave the house?* God knew the answers I needed. "Yes, I *can* live independently."

I took off my sleep shades and twirled the elastic in my hand. God, in his wisdom, was giving me time to adjust before my only option would be to depend on sound, the flow of traffic, and non-visual cues, all of which I was learning right now.

"It's the same world," I said thinking back to my first lesson. "I'll handle the things I can see visually and the ones I can't non-visually. Right, Bob?" I wanted to move forward, or would that be north? Well, I still had time to figure that out.

While Bob and Rita chatted, God gave me a wonderful verse to savor.

I will lead the blind by ways they have not known,
Along unfamiliar paths I will guide them;

Isaiah 42:16, NIV.

Nothing was perfect. But God Himself had blessed me by surrounding me with encouraging people, especially Bob, who showed me what I was capable of doing.

God did this for me because he loves me *that* much.

ACKNOWLEDGEMENTS

Without the following influences and help in my life, you wouldn't be reading this book. I am so grateful to:

God—who instilled in me a passion for this topic and confidence to write out my story and share it with the world.

Members of the Bureau of Blindness and Visual Services for their empathy and understanding, problem-solving skills, and the training they provided me in 2009 and during various periods in 2010-11. This isn't the kind of caring one can manufacture. They have an important role that changes lives.

My family had to put their needs on hold for awhile as I banged out words on my keyboard. Everyone worked together, from my mother and brother who waited on dinner sometimes because I got lost in my writing, to my niece, who waited on her husband, Mike, too many times to count as he helped me when my computer revolted against me. Everyone in the family encouraged me. I'm thankful for their patience.

My friends—Bettie-Lou, Sue, Kathy, Lynn, Vicki, Frank, and the real Julio, all encouraged me and let me brainstorm with them as I fleshed out various scenes. They've also been there for me as I adjusted to my blindness training and later, wrote this book.

My prayer warriors—a group of ten or so Christ-centered people who faithfully prayed for my needs and progress in my writing ministry. They provided physical resources for my office and offered support by attending my speaking endeavors.

Aldine Hecker—a special sister in faith. She has prayed for my faith and safety in my travels overseas and promoted my writing for over thirty years. She's the first one I go to when I have problems and the first one I share with when blessings come my way.

RJ Thesman—my editor and dear writing colleague who walked me through this book by bringing clarity to my experiences. She removed the "can't" from my vocabulary and replaced it with "how long" and "when."

My local chapter of Pennwriters—members of my critique group who asked me questions about my experience and helped me fill in the missing pieces. They rallied around to help me shape this book with their insights, laughter, and encouragement. I couldn't have done it without them.

Sarah Kay Gamble—the photographer who checked for good weather days and fit two wonderful photoshoots into her busy schedule.

Heather Desuta—the book designer who, in short order, put her skills to good use and made my book cover and pages look compelling.

Special Thanks—to all those who reviewed my book before it came out and encouraged me with their responses.

About the Author

Amy is a vision-impaired Christian author and speaker. When she was 28, doctors diagnosed her with Retinitis Pigmentosa (RP)—a degenerative eye-disease that eventually causes blindness. Later, she developed Usher's Syndrome, which causes deafness.

Having taught in Latin America, South East Asia and the Middle East, Amy often features glimpses of these and other cultures in her writing.

Amy blogs about the challenges she faces as she loses more vision and hearing. But more importantly, she shares the lessons God reveals to her through her difficulties. You can read about her experiences on her blog— www.amybovaird.com.